Historic Resource Facilities

First published in the United Sates of America by
Rockport Publishers, Inc.
33 Commercial Street
Gloucester, Massachusetts 01930-5089
Telephone 508 282 9590

Distribution by
Rockport Publishers
Gloucester, Massachusetts

ISBN 1-56496-225-3

10 9 8 7 6 5 4 3 2 1

EDITORIAL: Two Head Communications, Washington, D.C.
DESIGN: Group C, Inc.
LAYOUT: Jennie Bush, Books By Design, Inc.
PAGING: Irene Elios, Sherry Fatla
FRONT COVER PHOTOGRAPH: Dietrich Floeter Photography *(project appears on page 163)*
BACK COVER PHOTOGRAPHS: John Sutton Photography (top), Larry Olsen (middle),
        Vittoria Visuals (bottom)

Printed in Hong Kong

Historic Resource
Facilities

1997 Review

The American Institute of Architects Press

Washington, D.C.

Contents

1997 Jury

CHARLES ATHERTON, FAIA, is a registered architect and past president of the Washington Chapter of the AIA. Since 1965 he has headed the staff of the Commission of Fine Arts, an independent federal agency that has primary responsibility for design review of public buildings, monuments, parks, and historic districts in Washington, D.C. He also serves on the Committee to Develop a Comprehensive Design Plan for the White House, is chairman of the Historic American Buildings Survey Foundation, and is a member of the board of the Historical Society of Washington.

JERRY L. BERGGREN, AIA, is principal-in-charge of historic preservation and restoration projects for Berggren & Woll, Architects, in Lincoln, Nebraska. He is active in many preservation organizations, including the National Trust for Historic Preservation, the Association for Preservation Technology International, and the Nebraska State Historical Society. He is president of the Nebraska Preservation Council and serves on the Lincoln/Lancaster County Preservation Commission. He has been a member of the AIA Committee on Historic Resources since 1979.

HUGH C. MILLER, FAIA, is a registered architect with varied experience in planning and architectural projects and the development of state, national, and international preservation programs. He has worked as an architect and planner in private practice and for the federal government and the Commonwealth of Virginia. He served as the first director of the Virginia Department of Historic Resources and as state historic preservation officer from 1989 to 1994. As part of his twenty-eight-year career with the National Park Service, he served as chief historical architect from 1979 to 1988. He is now a professor of historic preservation at Goucher College, where he teaches building technology. Mr. Miller has been active in the movement to preserve historic landscapes and was made an honorary member of the American Society of Landscape Architects in recognition of his efforts in this field. A member and past chairman of the AIA Committee on Historic Resources, he currently chairs the group's *Review* subcommittee.

SHARON COLLINS PARK, AIA, is the senior historical architect at the Heritage Preservation Services office of the National Park Service. She has written and lectured on numerous technical preservation topics, including deterioration of materials, accessibility for persons with disabilities, lead-based paint and other health hazards, affordable housing, and design approaches within historic districts. She has served as preservation advisor to federal, state, and local agencies.

Jury Comments

From the renaissance of historic homes, libraries, and commercial spaces, to large, long-term, highly complex projects such as the renovation of the Michigan or Texas state capitols, this book presents the state of the architectural profession as it relates to historic preservation and attests that preservation architecture is both exciting and important. The fifty-seven projects featured in this book maintain a sense of appreciation for and understanding of the past, and recognize the need for incorporating modern technology within these historic spaces. Careful renovation, restoration, and preservation enhance not only the buildings themselves, but the neighborhoods and communities that surround them by ensuring a secure future for these architecturally significant emblems of the past.

Large or small, individual private residences or important public structures, the common characteristic among these projects is their diversity. Three categories of work—restoration, renovation, and special projects—only begin to define them. Several building types and two approaches with special considerations—long-term and scholarly projects—can be found in these pages. Long-term projects are generally costly and intricate, addressing the needs of large public buildings. These projects reach completion after decades of work, changes of administration, and sometimes without substantial initial support; but as such projects continue, public sentiment and support grow. Many of these structures are now sources of great community pride. Four projects in this review represent scholarly restoration, pure restoration that re-creates original methods down to the detail of crafting materials on site. The projects, fascinating in their attention to accuracy, often take place over many years with results that reflect preservation in the truest sense.

Courthouses

In nearly every county in the United States, one can find a courthouse presiding over the public green, standing as the physical embodiment of justice. Four of the five courthouse projects selected are county courthouse renovations. The fifth, the Byron White U.S. Courthouse in Denver, is home to the U.S. Court of Appeals, Tenth Circuit, and the U.S. District Court. The county courthouse renovations, from the 1884 Victorian-style Gloucester County Courthouse in New Jersey to the 1931 Art Deco Ramsey County Courthouse and St. Paul City Hall in Minnesota, seamlessly incorporate modern security, accessibility, mechanical systems, and technology into the historic fabric of these structures. The Westmoreland County Courthouse in Pennsylvania highlights the use of appropriate materials with the selection of a cast-aluminum dome to replace the original terra-cotta structure.

Cultural Facilities

Along with libraries, cultural facilities speak to both the public and the private commitment to the arts. Whether a local community theater or the National Gallery of Art, preservation of suitable structures for the arts has strong public support. Four of the seven projects in this category are performing-art spaces. Of those, three—the Warner Theater in Washington, D.C., the American Conservatory Theater in San Francisco, and Jordan Hall at the New England Conservatory of Music in Boston—were originally built as theaters. Gilroy Old City Hall in Gilroy, California, is a rehabilitated town hall. These theaters have been beautifully restored, each in

a different style and each deserving the reader's attentive review. In reviewing these particular structures, keep in mind the challenge of incorporating modern acoustics to make these structures as technically advanced as they are aesthetically pleasing.

Two cultural facility projects are large national museums: the National Gallery of Art and the National Building Museum, both in Washington, D.C. These projects focus on creating and improving gallery space for their collections. The National Gallery needed additional space; the National Building Museum requirements were more mechanical in nature. The Academy of the Arts in Easton, Maryland, represents the quintessential regional arts center, combining a historic school and adjacent house into a fully renovated 20,000-square-foot facility.

Educational Facilities

Of the eight educational facilities featured here, all but one represent higher education. Georgetown Visitation School in Washington, D.C., is a secondary school. The reasons for renovation or restoration of these facilities are wide ranging: a devastating fire, weathering conditions that caused extensive damage, seismic reinforcement, and the need for additional, state-of-the-art classroom and administrative spaces. Each project is interesting and well-executed. In particular, the jury notes the fascinating techniques employed at Building 01-020 on the Stanford University campus to ensure appropriate seismic reinforcement, and at the Whig and Clio Halls on the campus of Princeton University, where a unique clamping system enabled monolithic columns to be lifted so their bases and plinths could be removed and replaced.

Libraries

Six libraries and research centers, not affiliated with an educational facility, are included in the review. Special consideration is given to the Parlin Memorial Library in Everett, Massachusetts, because of its integration into a dense urban site. The addition, while compatible with the original structure, is modern in its use of color and detail. The Howell Carnegie Library in Howell, Michigan, is exemplary for its integration of barrier-free access at the main entrance. The Center for Motion Picture Study in Beverly Hills, which began its life as a water-treatment plant, presents an interesting example of adaptive reuse. The Williams Research Center in New Orleans was originally a court building, constructed in 1915. Four of the projects included an addition as well as restoration work, demonstrating that the public library in America is alive and well.

Municipal Facilities

Municipal buildings represented include two city halls and the Danville Municipal Building in Virginia, which incorporates a police station as well. The Philadelphia City Hall is a long-term restoration project whose initiation alone required four years of planning. Work on the first phase of the building will not be completed until 1999. Oakland City Hall, built in 1914, is the first high-rise building to be fitted with base isolators to dissipate the seismic energy of earthquakes.

Office and Mixed-Use Facilities

Seven office buildings and mixed-use facilities were selected. The renovation of the metal support system for the Chicago Tribune Building, built in 1925, involved difficult work, mostly done at night, that was closely monitored by the National Park Service. The architectural team for the Rookery met the challenge of incorporating the most significant elements of the building's three major periods—the original 1888 Burnham & Root design, the 1905 Wright remodeling, and the 1930 Drummond remodeling—into a unified whole. The Pacific Gas and Electric Company, in San Francisco, involved a seismic retrofit and the combining of four separate sites into a single complex. The preservation of the Second Empire-style Old Executive Office Building in Washington, D.C., was completed in March 1995 after more than ten years of work.

Residential Projects

The three residential projects included in this volume represent the full spectrum of restoration: from elaborate to simple and from strict preservation and conservation to sensitive addition. The eighteenth-century Pennock Farmstead, Quaker-built and abandoned in the 1960s, was meticulously and faithfully restored for use as a private residence. The addition of a small turret to a 1908 private home in Chicago's Hutchinson Street Historic Landmark District continued a tradition of fine craftsmanship through attention to scale and materials. The restoration of the Governor's Residence in Utah, destroyed by fire in 1993, included restoring elegant finishes and incorporating seismic upgrades.

Special Projects

Without a plan, many large projects that are executed over a long period of time may deteriorate or lose their initial focus. That is why the *Illustrated Guidelines for Rehabilitating Buildings at the Presidio of San Francisco* is important. The guidelines coordinate local and national guidelines and have implications for universities, communities, and Federal agencies. Plans and guides are important tools for preservation architects and are often overlooked in publications. In an effort to present a thorough review of preservation work, guidelines such as those presented in this book are important.

The re-creation of five chandeliers at the Biltmore Hotel in Coral Gables, Florida, serves as a reminder that the scope and scale of a project are not the final measure of its value, but rather the attention and thought that are brought to it.

The one religious structure featured, the Plum Street Temple in Cincinnati, Ohio, was completed in two phases: the first focused on the exterior and the second on completing the intricate interior, which is stenciled with patterns in more than forty colors.

Two public buildings are among the special projects noted for their attention to technical requirements. The Memorial Amphitheater in Arlington National Cemetery was selected for its use of waterproofing technology, and the new facade for the Internal Revenue Service Building on Pennsylvania Avenue is a long-awaited and wonderful addition to the historic Federal Triangle complex.

Scholarly projects, all of them national treasures, include Thomas Jefferson's home, Monticello; his mountain retreat, Poplar Forest; the University of Virginia Academical Village; and a meticulous reconstruction of the treading barn at George Washington's Mount Vernon. The hallmark of these scholarly works is years of research, which are invested in creating a final product that is near to the original and that go beyond the buildings themselves to capture the milieu of the site and era in which they were constructed.

State Capitols

Long-term projects are exercises in patience, requiring the architect to devote years to realizing programmatic goals while working with many different people, administrations, and ideas. The Michigan State Capitol, New Jersey State House Capitol Complex, Pennsylvania State Capitol, and Texas State Capitol are highly successful

examples of long-term projects. It is important to remember that the finishes are only one small part of the overall project. Mechanical, security, and technological requirements all must be addressed through upgrades and improvements.

Transportation

Most of the transportation projects in this volume have resulted in the revival of great rail stations of the past for contemporary use: Amtrak's 30th Street Station in Philadelphia; Depot Plaza in Lafayette, Indiana; and the Danville, Virginia, Rail Passenger Station. One unique project, the Angels™ Flight funicular railway in Los Angeles, connects Bunker Hill with the city's financial district. Originally built in 1901, the railway was completely refurbished in 1996, including the station house, incline cars, trestle, tracks, and arch.

Amtrak's 30th Street Station involved interior and exterior improvements, mechanical upgrades, and commercial revitalization. Depot Plaza is an intermodal transportation facility, and Danville does double-duty as a passenger station and a regional science center. Both Depot Plaza and Danville received funding through the Intermodal Surface Transportation Efficiency Act's Transportation Enhancements Program.

The Reading Terminal Train Shed in Philadelphia opened in March 1994 as the ballroom in the city's convention center. The terminal's former life is recalled by the use of stainless steel tracks in the floor and marble-clad pylons that suggest the bumpers that once stopped train cars.

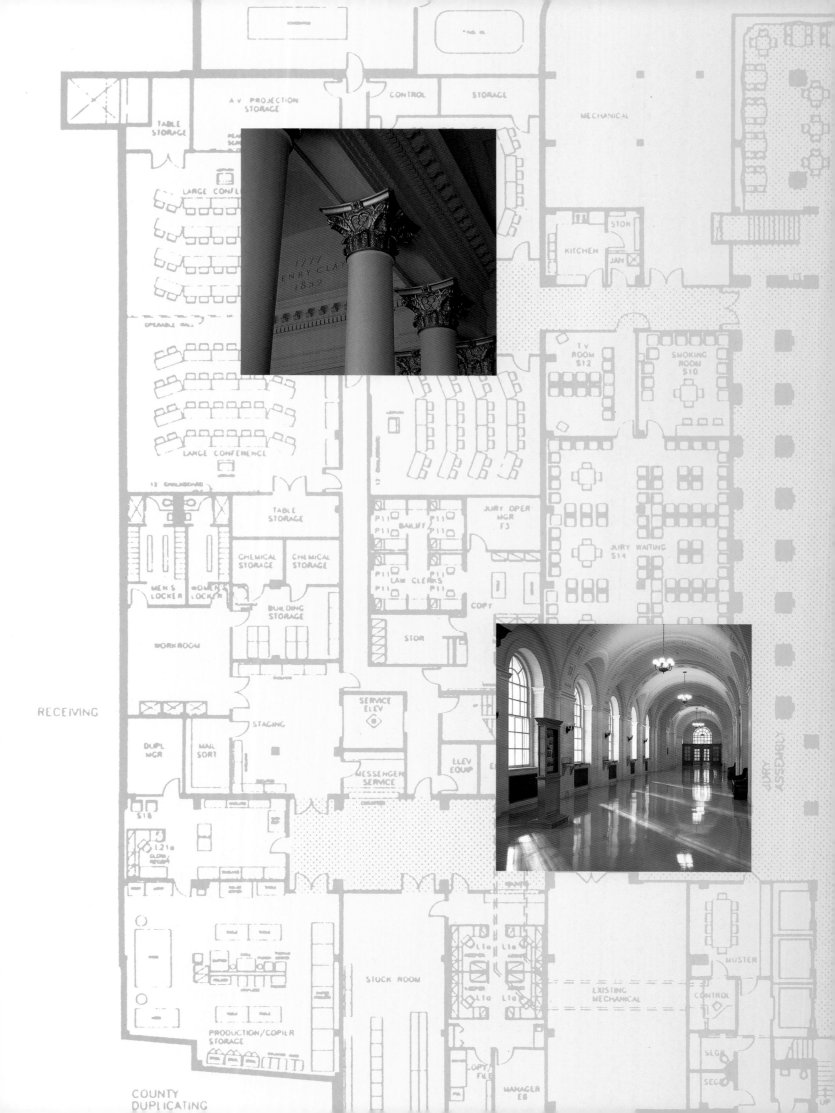

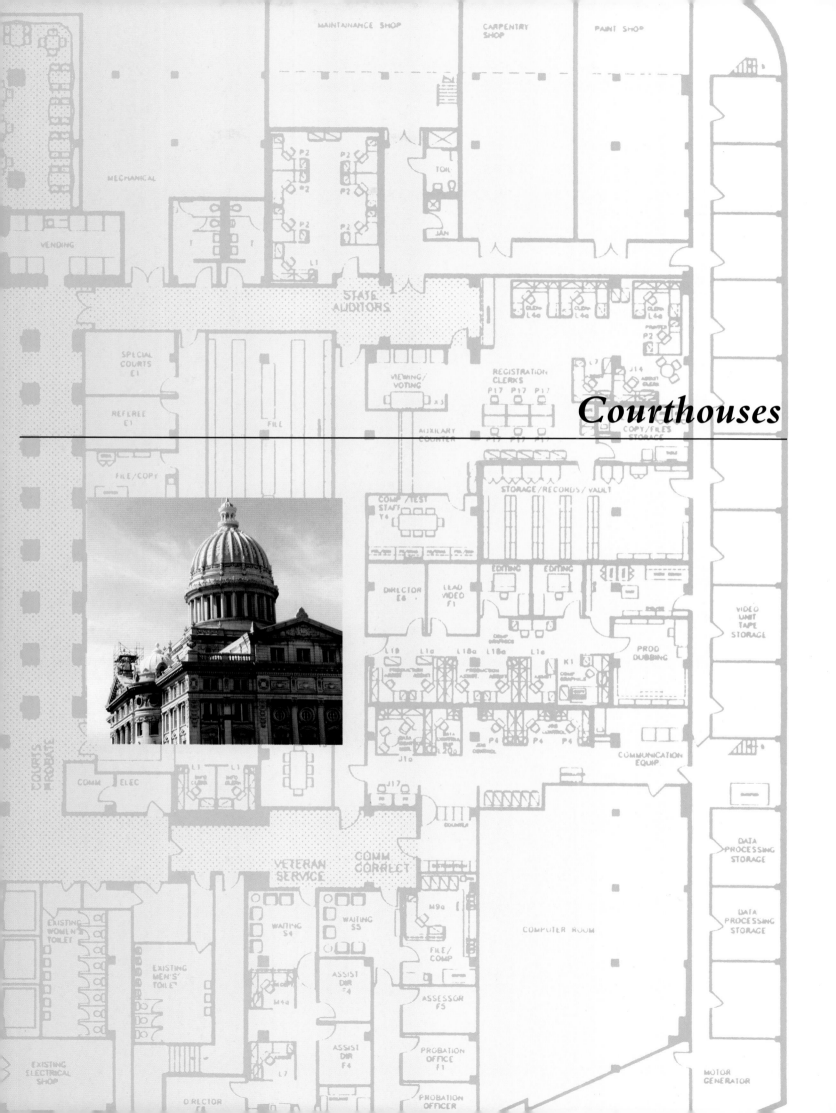

Courthouses

Byron White U.S. Courthouse
Denver, Colorado

Michael Barber Architecture

Originally built circa 1910 to house the district and appellate courts, the main post office, and all other federal agencies in the city, the building had lost much of its Neoclassic grandeur through architecturally insensitive remodeling. The design direction for this project was to restore the exterior and important interior public spaces in a historically accurate manner and to rehabilitate and modernize the remainder of the building to serve exclusively as a Federal courthouse.

The original design drawings of Tracy, Swartwout, and Litchfield, and detailed photographs aided in accurate restoration of public spaces. Redesigned spaces were executed in a manner sensitive to the history and function of the building. The project added to the body of restoration and decorative craft technology. For example, much was learned about successful restoration of pure white marble. New specifications and details were developed to define monumental woodwork.

Owner
General Services
Administration, Region Eight

Data

Type of Facility
Federal courthouse

Type of Construction
Rehabilitation and restoration

Historic Status
National Register of Historic
Places

Area of Building
244,000 GSF

Total Project Cost
$28 million

Status of Project
Completed July 1994

Credits

Architect of Record
Michael Barber Architecture
303 16th Street, Suite 300
Denver, Colorado 80202

Structural Engineer
Martin/Martin, Inc.
Wheatbridge, Colorado

Mechanical/Electrical Engineer
Cator Ruma & Associates
Lakewood, Colorado

Historic Preservation Consultant
Long Hoeft Architects
Georgetown, Colorado

Acoustics Consultant
Cerami and Associates, Inc.
Long Island City, New York

Asbestos Consultant
Spence-Geiger
Associates, Inc.
Golden, Colorado

Cost Estimating Consultant
Associated Construction
Consultants, Inc.
Aurora, Colorado

Elevators Consultant
Lerch, Bates
& Associates, Inc.
Littleton, Colorado

(credits continue)

Credits (continued)

Graphics Consultant
Weber Design
Denver, Colorado

Soils Engineering Consultant
Maxim Technologies, Inc.
(formerly Chen-Northern, Inc.)
Denver, Colorado

Electrical Security Consultant
The RMH Group, Inc.
Lakewood, Colorado

Waterproofing/Stone Consultant
Wiss, Janney, Elstner
Associates, Inc.
Wheat Ridge, Colorado

Historic Structures Report Consultant
MAHG Architecture, Inc.
(formerly Matt Mobley
McGowan & Griffin, P.A.:
Architects)
Fort Smith, Arkansas

Survey Consultant
C. R. Moore Surveying
Arvada, Colorado

Lab Testing Consultant
CTC-Geotek, Inc.
Denver, Colorado

Specifications Consultant
ASCS
Denver, Colorado

Contractor
Dawson Construction
Gadsden, Alabama

Photographer
R. Greg Hursley
Austin, Texas

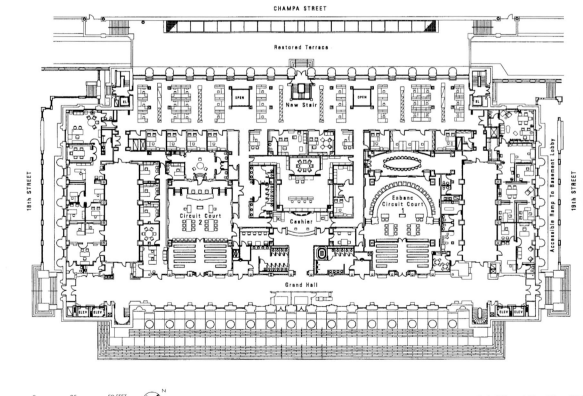

Rehabilitated First Floor Plan

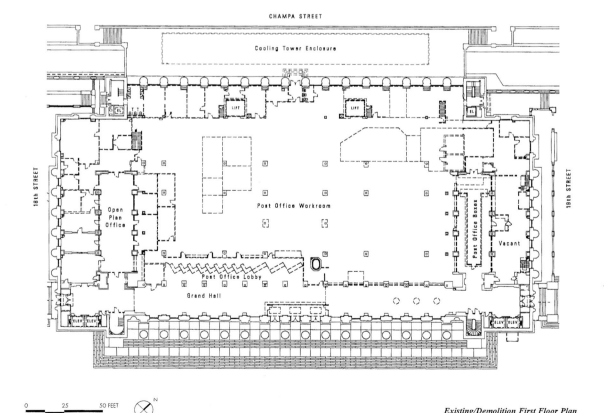

CHAMPA STREET

Cooling Tower Enclosure

Post Office Workroom

Open Plan Office

Post Office Boxes

Vacant

Post Office Lobby

Grand Hall

18th STREET

19th STREET

0   25   50 FEET

Existing/Demolition First Floor Plan

Gloucester County Courthouse
Woodbury, New Jersey

Vitetta Group

ARCHITECT'S STATEMENT

Restoration plans for the 1884 Victorian-style county courthouse and the adjacent 1930 county building included improved accessibility throughout the complex and updating of certain heating/ventilation/air-conditioning and electrical systems. Through historical research, comprehensive master planning, and architectural, engineering, and restoration design services, the building was restored to a high standard, meeting all of the client's goals with a design that is historically compatible with the original design.

Owner
Gloucester County Board of
Chosen Freeholders

Data

Type of Facility
County courthouse

Type of Construction
Restoration

Historic Status
Contributing structure in a
National Register Historic
District

Area of Building
48,762 GSF

Total Project Cost
$3 million

Status of Project
Completed May 1995

Credits

Architect of Record/
Structural/Mechanical/
Electrical Engineer
Vitetta Group
53 Haddonfield Road,
Suite 306
Cherry Hill, New Jersey 08002

Contractor
Pilgrim Construction Co.
Cherry Hill, New Jersey

Photographers
Tom Crane Photography
Bryn Mawr, Pennsylvania

Joanne Bening
Philadelphia, Pennsylvania

Jack D. Neith
Mount Laurel, New Jersey

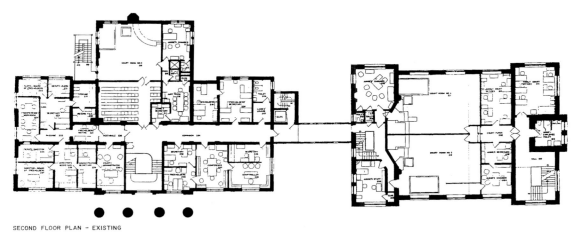

SECOND FLOOR PLAN - EXISTING

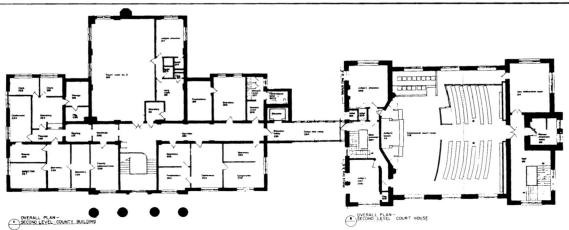

OVERALL PLAN -
SECOND LEVEL COUNTY BUILDING

OVERALL PLAN -
SECOND LEVEL COURT HOUSE

SCALE: 1·8" = 1'-0"

Ingham County Courthouse

Mason, Michigan

Wigen, Tincknell, Meyer & Associates, Inc.

ARCHITECT'S STATEMENT

In 1979 the Ingham County Commission committed to restoring the courthouse as a functioning seat of government while retaining the building's historic character and restoring missing elements. Restoration was completed sixteen years later, a statement of the county's commitment to restoring this structure. The county initially approached the restoration as a pay-as-you-go project. Small projects were completed through this process. The county finally decided, at the urging of the architect, that bonds should be sold to complete the remaining major portions of the restoration.

Exterior restoration included reconstruction of major portions of the clock tower, masonry rehabilitation, new slate roofing, and replication of removed dormers and balustrades. Interior restoration addressed code and barrier-free access issues as well as functional programming. The building was retrofitted with new heating, ventilation, and air conditioning systems, plumbing, electrical, and communications technology wiring. All woodwork was refinished, and decorative painting was reinstated in selected areas.

Owner
County of Ingham

Data
Type of Facility
County courthouse

Type of Construction
Restoration

Historic Status
National Register of Historic Places

Area of Building
31,620 GSF

Total Project Cost
$3.2 million

Status of Project
Completed August 1995

Credits
Architect of Record
Wigen, Tincknell, Meyer & Associates, Inc.
1647 South Washington Avenue
Saginaw, Michigan 48601

Structural Engineer
MacMillan Associates, Inc.
Bay City, Michigan

Mechanical/Electrical Engineer
Engineering Applications, Inc.
Lansing, Michigan

Contractor
Heartland Professional Construction Services, Inc.
(now merged with Clark Construction)
Lansing, Michigan

Photographer
Dietrich Floeter Photography
Traverse City, Michigan

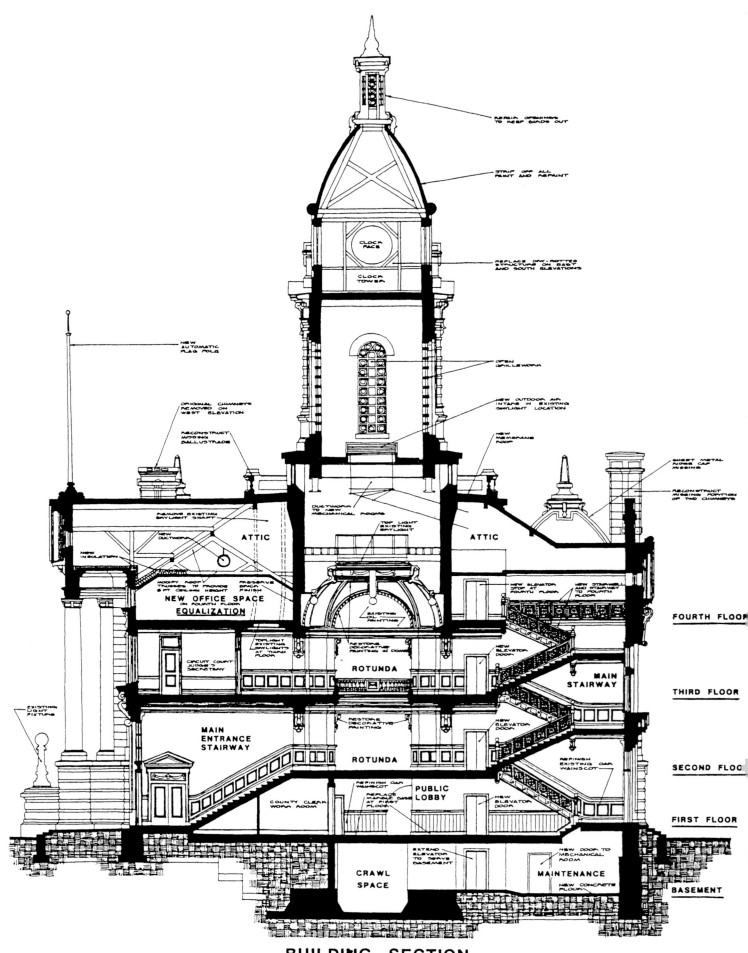

BUILDING SECTION

Ramsey County Courthouse and St. Paul City Hall

St. Paul, Minnesota

Wold Architects & Engineers

ARCHITECT'S STATEMENT

The existing courthouse and city hall, completed in 1931, is a premier example of Art Deco high-rise architecture. Major objectives of the 1994 addition, renovation, and restoration included functional improvements, the addition of state-of-the-art mechanical and technology systems, implementation of current life-safety and accessibility standards, and the creation of an addition consistent with the original architect's master plan.

A master plan was developed to meet the programmatic and restoration goals of the city, county, and courts, as well as the U.S. Secretary of the Interior's *Standards for Rehabilitation*. The most significant public spaces became the focus of the restoration and preservation efforts. A new interpretive area on the concourse level features an exhibit of building artifacts. Secondary historic spaces were modified to meet programmatic requirements, and new public lobby and reception areas were developed in keeping with the building's original character. Even in the building's least public areas, subtle detailing and furnishing help tie together the historic and reinterpreted areas of the building.

Area of Building
371,000 GSF

Total Project Cost
$46 million

Status of Project
Completed June 1994

Credits
Architect of Record
Wold Architects & Engineers
6 West Fifth Street
St. Paul, Minnesota 55102

Associate Architect
The Architectural Alliance
400 Clifton Avenue South
Minneapolis, Minnesota 55403

Historic Architect
Croxton Collaborative
1122 Madison Avenue
New York, New York 10028

Structural Engineer
Meyer, Borgman & Johnson, Inc.
Minneapolis, Minnesota

Mechanical/Electrical Engineer
Michaud Cooley Erickson &
Associates
Minneapolis, Minnesota

Programming Consultant
Carter Goble Associates
Columbia, South Carolina

Justice Consultant
Justice Planning Associates,Inc.
Columbia, South Carolina

Contractor
PCL Construction Services
Bloomington, Minnesota

Photographer
George Heinrich
Minneapolis, Minnesota

Owner
Ramsey County and the City of
St. Paul

Data
Type of Facility
County courthouse and city hall

Type of Construction
Restoration and rehabilitation

Historic Status
National Register of Historic
Places
Local landmark

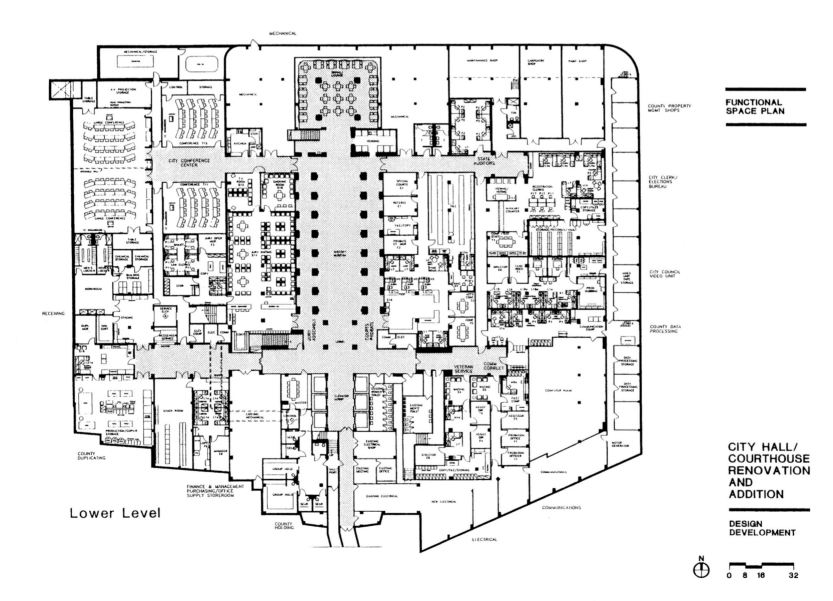

Lower Level

CITY HALL/
COURTHOUSE
RENOVATION
AND
ADDITION

DESIGN
DEVELOPMENT

N

0   8   16   32

Westmoreland County Courthouse

Greensburg, Pennsylvania

Wiss, Janney, Elstner Associates, Inc.

ARCHITECT'S STATEMENT

Westmoreland County Courthouse, designed by William Kauffman in 1908, is surmounted by a dome rising 175 feet above the ground. In the 1970s, the original terra-cotta of the dome was replaced with new terra-cotta that failed within ten years. Studies of potential substitute materials performed by the architect resulted in the selection of cast aluminum for reconstruction of the dome, designed to match its original appearance. A special structural subframe allowed each cast-aluminum panel to be supported independently from the original steel structure, permitting rapid installation using fasteners exposed on the interior for ease of future maintenance.

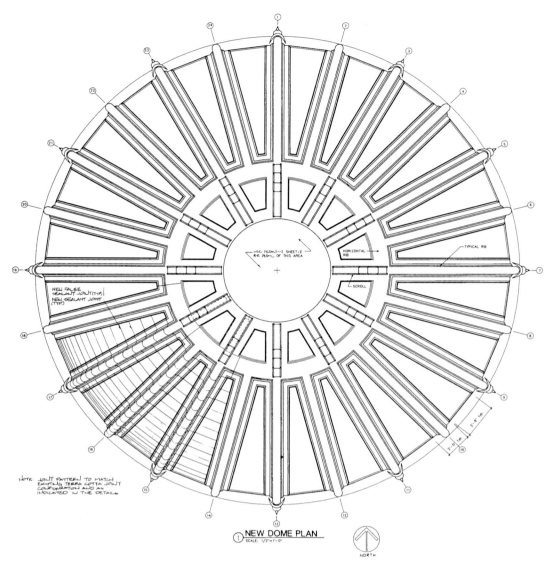

NOTE: JOINT PATTERN TO MATCH EXISTING TERRA COTTA JOINT CONFIGURATION AND AS INDICATED IN THE DETAILS

1 NEW DOME PLAN
  SCALE: 1/2"=1'-0"

NORTH

Owner
Westmoreland County
Commissioners

Data
Type of Facility
County courthouse

Type of Construction
Special project

Historic Status
National Register of Historic
Places

Area of Building
70,000 GSF

Total Project Cost
$2.225 million

Status of Project
Completed January 1993

Credits
*Architect of Record / Structural
Engineer*
Wiss, Janney, Elstner
Associates, Inc.
29 North Wacker Drive,
Suite 555
Chicago, Illinois 60606

Contractor
George Danko, Inc.
Latrobe, Pennsylvania

Photographer
Wiss, Janney, Elstner
Associates, Inc.
Chicago, Illinois

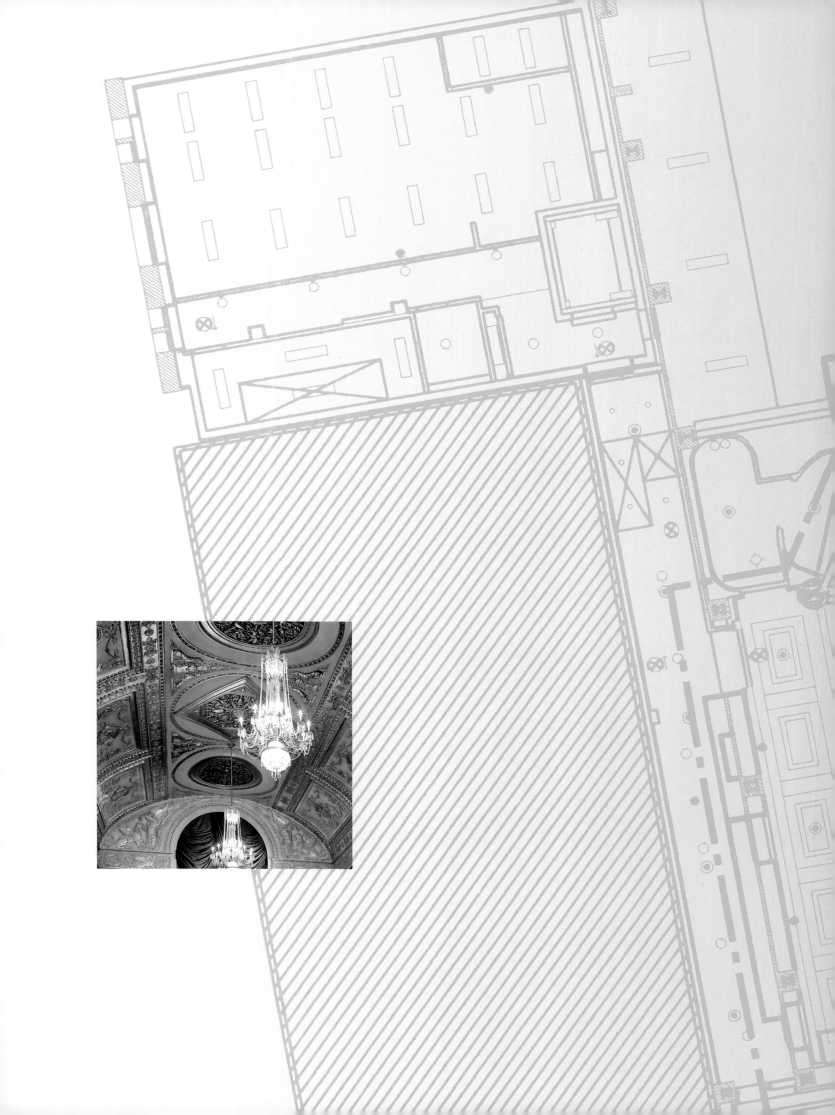

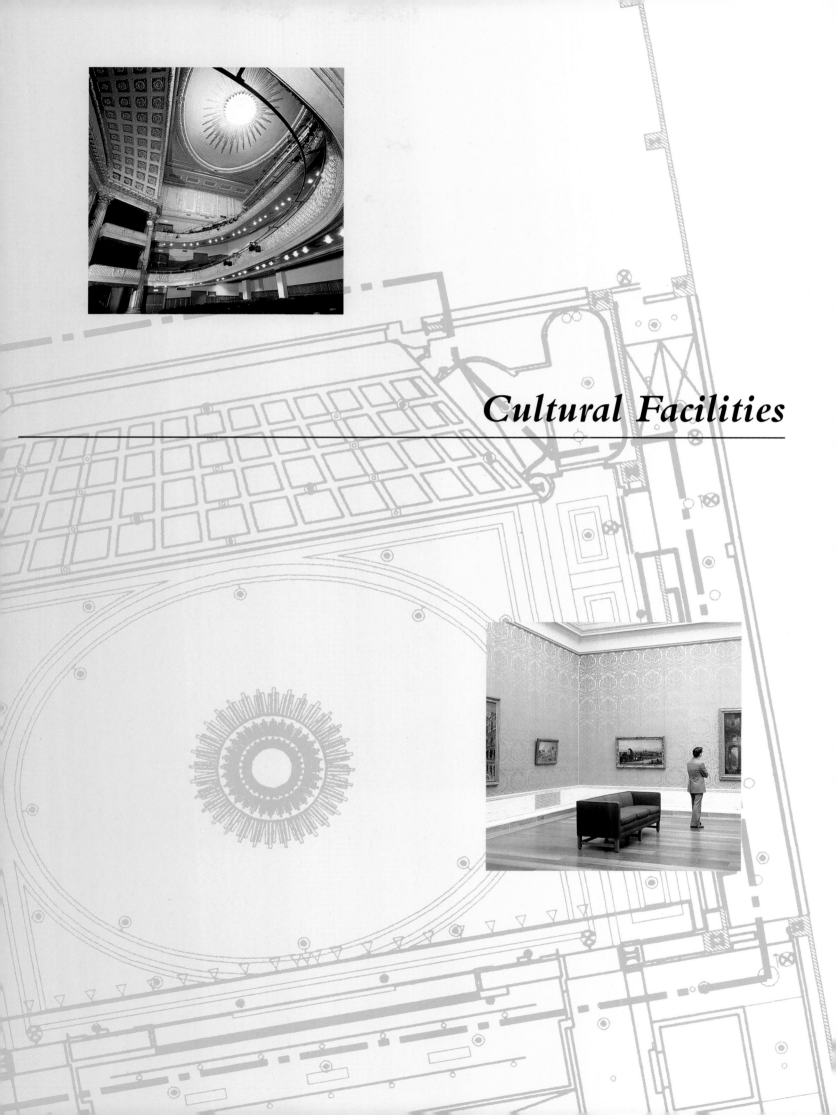

Cultural Facilities

Academy of the Arts

Easton, Maryland

Quinn Evans/Architects

ARCHITECT'S STATEMENT

Since 1960, the historic Easton Primary and Grammar School has been the identifying symbol for the Academy of the Arts. The 6,800-square-foot school consisted of a pair of wood-frame structures, one dating from the 1840s and one from the 1870s. To respond to the Academy's growing needs, an adjacent house of the same period was purchased. A design plan was crafted to rehabilitate the historic house and residence and construct a 10,000-square-foot addition linking the two. The new atrium links the first-floor galleries and second-floor classrooms, creating a central courtyard and sculpture garden.

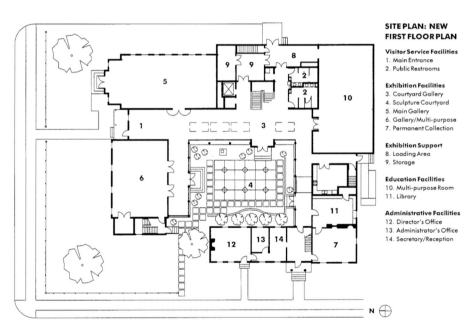

SITE PLAN: NEW FIRST FLOOR PLAN

Visitor Service Facilities
1. Main Entrance
2. Public Restrooms

Exhibition Facilities
3. Courtyard Gallery
4. Sculpture Courtyard
5. Main Gallery
6. Gallery/Multi-purpose
7. Permanent Collection

Exhibition Support
8. Loading Area
9. Storage

Education Facilities
10. Multi-purpose Room
11. Library

Administrative Facilities
12. Director's Office
13. Administrator's Office
14. Secretary/Reception

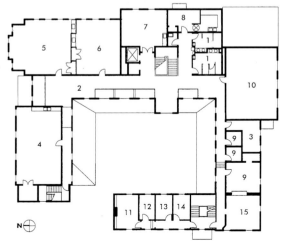

SECOND FLOOR PLAN

Visitor Service Facilities
1. Public Restrooms

Exhibition Facilities
2. Courtyard Gallery

Exhibition Support Areas
3. Storage

Education Facilities
4. Painting Studio
5. Drawing Studio
6. Children's Studio
7. Ceramics/Sculpture Studio
8. Photography Studio
9. Music Studio
10. Dance Studio

Administrative Facilities
11. Performing Arts Office
12. Education Office
13. Administrator's Office
14. Bookkeeper's Office
15. Support Staff's Office

Owner
Academy of the Arts

Data
Type of Facility
Regional public arts facility

Type of Construction
Rehabilitation

Historic Status
Contributing structure in a National Register Historic District

Area of Buildings
6,800 GSF (original building)
4,500 GSF (adjacent house)
10,000 GSF (addition)

Total Project Cost
$1.450 million (construction only)

Status of Project
Completed September 1991

Credits
Architect of Record
Quinn Evans/Architects
1214 28th Street, N.W.
Washington, D.C. 20007

Structural Engineer
FDE Ltd., Consulting Engineers
Alexandria, Virginia

Mechanical/Electrical Engineer
Smith & Faass Consulting Engineers
Germantown, Maryland

Contractor
Willow Construction Company
Easton, Maryland

Photographer
Larry Olsen
Washington, D.C.

Geary Theater Building, American Conservatory Theater

San Francisco, California

Gensler and Associates Architects and Page & Turnbull, Inc.

ARCHITECT'S STATEMENT

During the 1989 Loma Prieta earthquake, the proscenium and suspended lighting of the Geary Theater collapsed while other portions of the auditorium suffered plaster fracturing. The demands of the restoration encompassed the entire building, but specific attention was devoted to re-creating the Beaux Arts ornamental stenciling and gilded plasterwork on the interior. Relying on historic photographs, existing undamaged details, and drawings, skilled artisans were put to the test by local, state, and Federal quality standards. The success of the restoration confirms that high-quality artistic craftsmanship is still alive in San Francisco.

Historic Rendering. Though theater is now known by another name, this drawing was prepared by the building's original architects, Bliss and Faville, in about 1910.

Owner
American Conservatory Theater

Data
Type of Facility
Dramatic arts theater

Type of Construction
Restoration

Historic Status
National Register of Historic
Places
Local landmark

Area of Building
70,000 GSF

Total Project Cost
$23 million

Status of Project
Completed December 1995

Credits
Architect of Record
Gensler and Associates
Architects
600 California Street
San Francisco, California
94108

Historic Preservation Architect
Page & Turnbull, Inc.
724 Pine Street
San Francisco, California
94108

Structural Engineer
SOH & Associates
San Francisco, California

Mechanical Engineer
Guttmann & MacRitchie
San Francisco, California

Electrical Engineer
Cammisa & Wipf
San Francisco, California

Theater Consultant
Theatre Projects Consultants
Ridgefield, Connecticut

Contractor
Cahill Contractors
San Francisco, California

Photographer
Sharon Reisdorf
San Francisco, California
John Sutton Photography
San Francisco, California

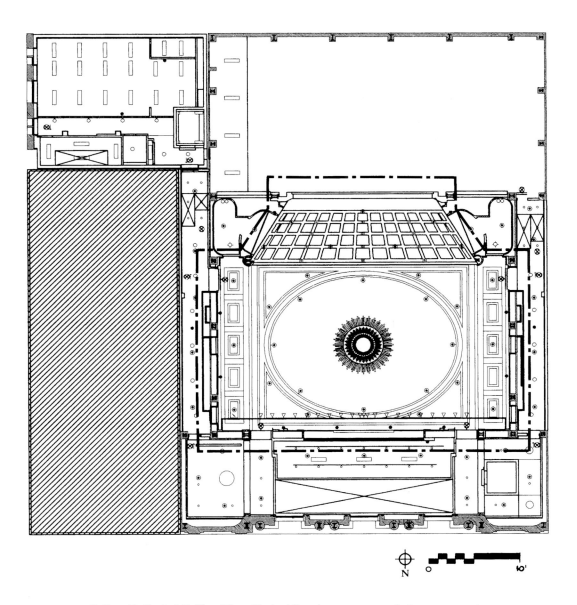

Gallery Reflected Ceiling Plan. Dashed line denotes extent of plaster restoration.

N   0   10'

Gilroy Old City Hall
Gilroy, California

Architectural Resources Group, Architects, Planners, & Conservators, Inc.

ARCHITECT'S STATEMENT

Gilroy's Old City Hall was dedicated in 1905 and served as the town hall until the 1980s, when a new city hall was constructed. The city currently leases the building to a tenant who operates it as a restaurant and theater. The structural components of Old City Hall, which sustained massive damage after the 1989 Loma Prieta earthquake, include unreinforced stone, three types of unreinforced brick, and wood framing. The design challenge was to arrive at a structural repair and bracing strategy that retained as much historic fabric as possible. The solution combined core drilling and the insertion of steel reinforcing rods; steel beams on west and south facades; and shotcrete, to which existing brick and stone were tied with concealed stainless-steel pins. The very rare Seth Thomas seven-day clock in the tower was restored and was restarted at 5:04 p.m. on October 17, 1994—exactly five years after the earthquake hit and the clock stopped—at a celebration to mark the reopening of Old City Hall.

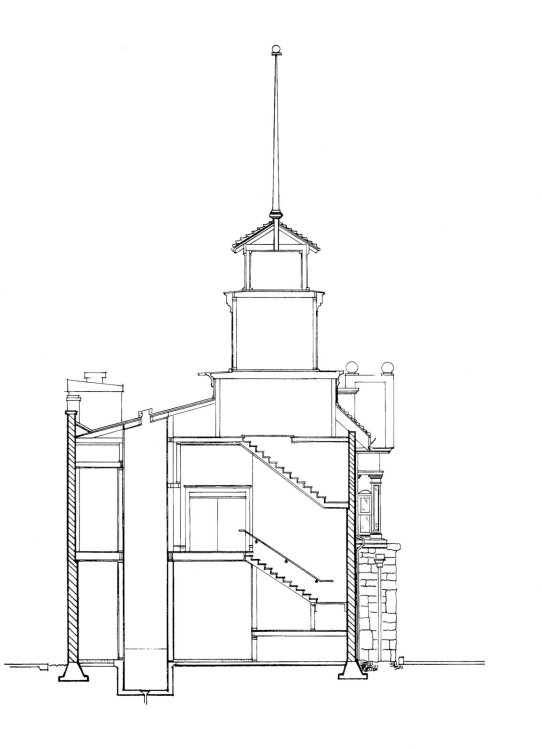

OLD CITY HALL
GILROY, CALIFORNIA

0   4   8   12   20

TRANSVERSE SECTION

O w n e r
City of Gilroy

D a t a
Type of Facility
Restaurant and community
theater

Type of Construction
Rehabilitation

Historic Status
National Register of Historic
Places
Local landmark

Area of Building
6,200 GSF

Total Project Cost
$2.2 million

Status of Project
Completed October 1994

C r e d i t s
Architect of Record
Architectural Resources Group,
Architects, Planners, &
Conservators, Inc.
Pier 9, The Embarcadero
San Francisco, California
94111

Structural Engineer
Meserve Engineering
Los Gatos, California

Contractor
HP Construction, General
Contractors
San Jose, California

Photographer
Bruce D. Judd
San Francisco, California

National Building Museum

Washington, D.C.

Karn Charuhas Chapman & Twohey

ARCHITECT'S STATEMENT

The project consisted of upgrading twenty exhibition galleries, the archives, and the educational and catering facilities. The most challenging task was to provide precise temperature and humidity controls in the galleries. The solution reconciled functional, historic, and aesthetic concerns by locating individual air-handling units in a new acoustically treated architectural enclosure in each gallery. These enclosures followed the configuration of the arches, creating a small vestibule to access the galleries from the Great Hall. The new design, which allows for future expansion and construction phasing to accommodate the museum's exhibit schedule, provides maximum exhibition space, preservation of existing views, and minimal intervention into the historic fabric of the building.

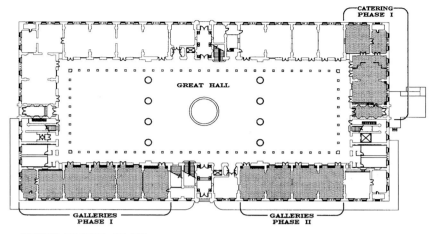

FIRST FLOOR PLAN

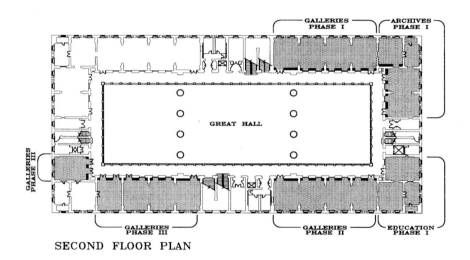

SECOND FLOOR PLAN

 Renovated Area  Acoustically Designed Architectural Enclosures

0 8 16 32 64

O w n e r
General Services Administration

D a t a
Type of Facility
Museum

Type of Construction
Rehabilitation

Historic Status
National Historic Landmark

Area of Project
33,000 GSF

Total Project Cost
$1.1 million

Status of Project
Completed December 1995

C r e d i t s
Architect of Record
Karn Charuhas Chapman & Twohey
1150 17th Street, N.W., Suite 103
Washington, D.C. 20036

Structural Engineer
Johns & Bhatia
Bethesda, Maryland

Mechanical/Electrical Engineer
Grotheer & Company
Washington, D.C.

Architectural Acoustics
Acoustical Design Collaborative, Ltd.
Falls Church, Virginia

Contractor
Marlowe Heating & Air Conditioning
Dunkirk, Maryland

Photographer
Hoachlander Photography Associates
Washington, D.C.

National Gallery of Art
Washington, D.C.

Vitetta Group

ARCHITECT'S STATEMENT

Initially constructed between 1937 and 1941 in the Neoclassical style, the National Gallery of Art's West Building in Washington, D.C., needed additional space to accommodate the museum's expanded collection and staff. Beginning in 1982, full architectural and engineering services have implemented several special projects at the museum to meet this need. Former art-storage vaults, a basketball court, and a lobby were transformed into new exhibition galleries, staff offices, and public spaces (the oculus), respectively, using similar materials and period details to seamlessly blend old and new. The multiphased plan also includes renovations to the main building's huge roof and skylight systems and restoration of the adjacent marble parapet walls. Public access was maintained during all construction phases.

Owner
    National Gallery of Art

Data
    Type of Facility
        Museum

    Type of Construction
        Special project

    Historic Status
        Contributing structure in a
        National Register Historic
        District
        Local landmark

    Area of Projects
        23,400 SF (interior)
        120,000 SF (daylight level)
        200,000 SF (roof)
        120,000 SF (skylights)
        25,000 SF (roof membrane)

    Area of Building
        935,000 GSF

    Total Project Cost
        Estimated through completion:
        $20 million

    Status of Project
        Estimated date of completion:
        1999

Credits
    *Architect of Record / Structural /
    Mechanical / Electrical Engineer*
        Vitetta Group
        1600 Duke Street, Suite 400
        Alexandria, Virginia 22314

    Contractors
        William V. Walsh Co., Inc.
        Rockville, Maryland

        Charles H. Tompkins Builders
        Washington, D.C.

        Associated Builders, Inc.
        Hyattsville, Maryland

        Brisk Waterproofing Co., Inc.
        Capitol Heights, Maryland

        Rand Construction Corp.
        Arlington, Virginia

    Photographer
        Jim H. Pipkin
        Washington, D.C.

The Mall

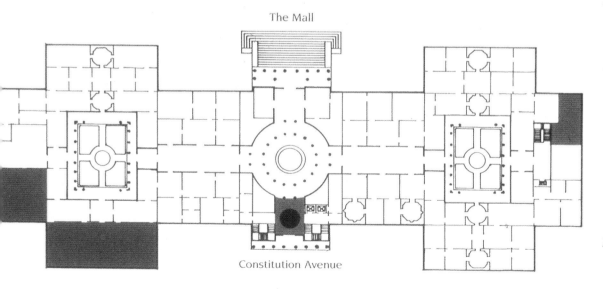

Constitution Avenue

National Gallery of Art
West Building

Jordan Hall, New England Conservatory of Music

Boston, Massachusetts

Ann Beha Associates, Inc.

ARCHITECT'S STATEMENT

This concert hall is a National Historic Landmark, renowned for its beauty, intimacy, and outstanding acoustics. The restoration provided the amenities required of a modern performance facility while retaining both acoustical and architectural quality. Key project features include restoration of the original design and integration of modern technology, incorporation of barrier-free access, and new audience amenities that serve the entire New England Conservatory of Music community. The project has been widely acclaimed by the Massachusetts Historical Commission, the Victorian Society in America, and the Boston Preservation Alliance.

Owner
New England Conservatory of Music

Data

Type of Facility
Concert hall on academic campus

Type of Construction
Restoration

Historic Status
National historic landmark
State and local landmark

Area of Building
100,000 GSF

Total Project Cost
$8.2 million

Status of Project
Completed October 1995

Credits

Architect of Record
Ann Beha Associates, Inc.
33 Kingston Street
Boston, Massachusetts 02111

Structural Engineer
LeMessurier Consultants, Inc.
Cambridge, Massachusetts

Mechanical/Electrical Engineer
R. G. Vanderweil Engineers, Inc.
Boston, Massachusetts

Acoustical and Sound System Consultant
R. Lawrence Kirkegaard and Associates
Downers Grove, Illinois

Theater Consultation and Stage Design
Charles Coster Theatre Design
New York, New York

Landscape Architect
Geller Associates
Boston, Massachusetts

Contractor
Walsh Brothers, Inc.
Cambridge, Massachusetts

Photographer
Wheeler Photographics
Weston, Massachusetts

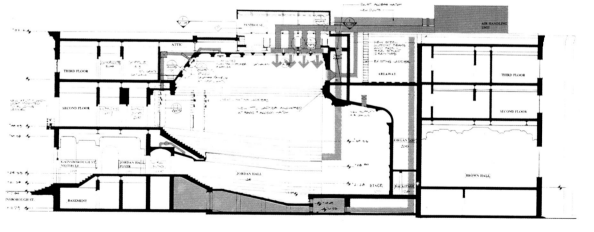

Longitudinal Section

KEY:
SUPPLY AIR
RETURN AIR

Warner Theater
Washington, D.C.

Shalom Baranes Associates, P.C.

ARCHITECT'S STATEMENT

When it was built in 1924, the Warner Theater was part of a thriving downtown theater district characterized by grand vaudeville and movie palaces. By 1987 the 2,500-seat venue had been in operation for nearly sixty years but was rundown and severely deficient in terms of modern codes and production requirements. The theater's elaborate public spaces were returned to their former grandeur. In many cases, finishes no longer in place were replicated, using techniques originally employed. Beyond the shell of the theater's house, all new service and support areas were constructed to provide state-of-the-art facilities. The building's terra-cotta facades were restored, and new exterior signage was installed. A new rooftop addition, housing three floors of office space, was designed to harmonize with the historic structure. The existing interior office space was fully renovated. All work was designed to the U.S. Secretary of the Interior's *Standards for Rehabilitation*.

Owner
The Kaempfer Company

Data

Type of Facility
Commercial theater

Type of Construction
Restoration

Historic Status
Eligible for the National
Register of Historic Places
Local landmark

Area of Building
70,000 GSF

Total Project Cost
$12 million

Status of Project
Completed 1993

Credits

Architect of Record
Shalom Baranes
Associates, P.C.
3299 K Street, N.W.,
Suite 400
Washington, D.C. 20007

Architect of Office Addition
Pei Cobb Freed and Partners
600 Madison Avenue
New York, New York 10022

Structural Engineer
Tadjer-Cohen-Edelson
Associates, Inc.
Silver Spring, Maryland

Mechanical/Electrical Engineer
GHT, Chartered
Arlington, Virginia

Theater Consultant
Roger Morgan Studio, Inc.
New York, New York

Historic Architectural Research
Traceries
Chevy Chase, Maryland

Acoustical Consultant
Klepper, Marshall, King
White Plains, New York

(credits continue)

Credits (continued)
Contractor
  OMNI Construction, Inc.
  Bethesda, Maryland

Photographer
  David Patterson
  Bethesda, Maryland

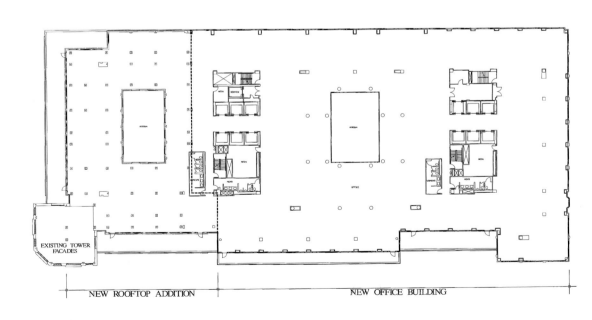

EXISTING TOWER FACADES

NEW ROOFTOP ADDITION   NEW OFFICE BUILDING

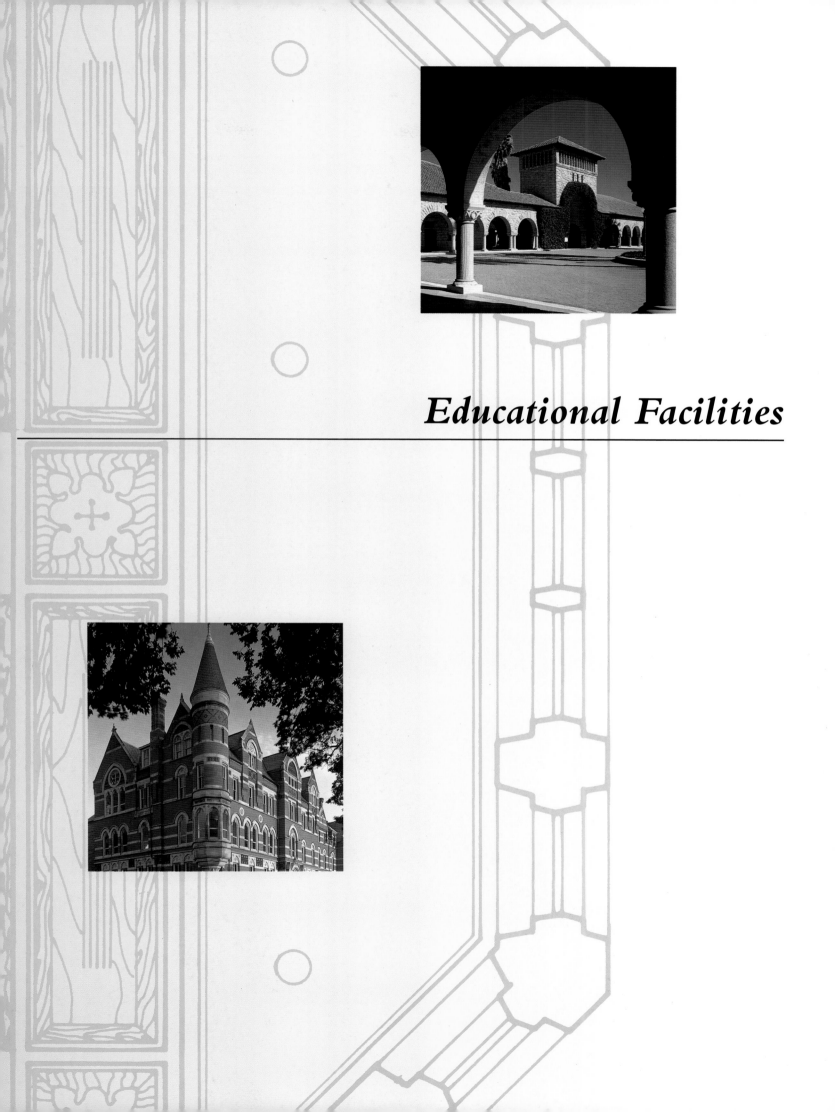

Educational Facilities

Sherzer Hall, Eastern Michigan University

Ypsilanti, Michigan

Quinn Evans/Architects

ARCHITECT'S STATEMENT

Built in 1903, the project is the university's second oldest classroom building. On March 9, 1989, more than fifty percent of the building was ravaged by fire. The reconstruction work was initiated just three months after the fire and was completed fourteen months later for the 1990 fall term.

Designed in a Romanesque Revival style, the masonry building consists of a center core with art studios at the four corners of each floor. Interior masonry walls and the original heavy timber structure, as well as mechanical, electrical, plumbing and fire-suppression systems, remain exposed and painted.

LEGEND
1. LOBBY
2. OBSERVATORY
3. MECHANICAL
4. OFFICE EXPANSION
5. EASEL PAINTING STUDIO
6. WATERCOLOR STUDIO
7. BEGINNING DRAWING STUDIO
8. BASEMENT

OWNER
Eastern Michigan University

DATA
Type of Facility
University classroom building

Type of Construction
Rehabilitation

Historic Status
Contributing structure in a
National Register Historic District

Area of Building
30,000 GSF

Total Project Cost
$5.6 million

Status of Project
Completed August 1990

CREDITS
Architect of Record
Quinn Evans/Architects
219 ½ North Main Street
Ann Arbor, Michigan 48104

Structural Engineer
Robert Darvas Associates
Ann Arbor, Michigan

Mechanical/Electrical Engineer
Gerald Potapa & Associates, Inc.
Madison Heights, Michigan

Lighting Design Consultant
Gary Steffy Lighting Design, Inc.
Ann Arbor, Michigan

Contractor
Turner Construction Company
Detroit, Michigan

Photographer
Fred Golden
Ann Arbor, Michigan

College Hall, Gallaudet University

Washington, D.C.

Einhorn Yaffee Prescott, Architecture & Engineering, P.C.

ARCHITECT'S STATEMENT

College Hall, a Victorian Gothic structure that is one of the university's oldest buildings, serves as the administrative hub of the campus. The design challenge was to remedy code deficiencies, poor mechanical and electrical services, deteriorated finishes, and accessibility problems; and to accommodate changing communication technologies while maintaining historic integrity.

Original room proportions, masonry partitions, and doorways emerged when additive remodelings were removed. New stained-glass windows, decorative tiles, and lighting were copied from whole or partial remnants. Up-to-date electrical, communications, and alarm systems were installed in soffits and baseboard raceways to manage future requirements. The building is now air conditioned for the first time, and steam radiators were replaced with a two-pipe fan coil system selected because of its small impact on the original architectural fabric. Existing window sashes were replaced with double-glazed replicas to improve insulation.

OWNER
Gallaudet University

DATA
Type of Facility
University administrative
building

Type of Construction
Rehabilitation

Historic Status
Eligible for the National
Register of Historic Places

Area of Building
48,900 GSF

Total Project Cost
$4.5 million

Status of Project
Completed July 1992

CREDITS
*Architect of Record/Mechanical and
Electrical Engineer/Interiors*
Einhorn Yaffee Prescott,
Architecture & Engineering, P.C.
1000 Potomac Street, N.W.
Washington, D.C. 20007

Structural Engineer
MMP International
Washington, D.C.

Contractor
Donohoe Construction
Company
Washington, D.C.

Photographers
Walter Smalling, Jr.
Washington, D.C.

Hameed Gorani
Gaithersburg, Maryland

Chris Barnes
Breman, Maine

Founder's Hall, Georgetown Visitation Preparatory School

Washington, D.C.

KressCox Associates, P.C.

ARCHITECT'S STATEMENT

Founded in 1799, this private secondary school is the oldest Catholic school for young women in America. In July 1993 the school suffered a devastating loss when a fire virtually destroyed Founder's Hall, its most significant campus structure. Built in 1873, this five-story Victorian landmark had served as the campus gateway for 120 years. Within the salvaged masonry exterior walls, the building was entirely reconstructed to achieve a balance between historic preservation of the exterior envelope, historic reconstruction of parlors and reception halls on the first floor, and construction of modern classrooms on the upper levels, ensuring the school's link with its past.

KEY

3 VENDING ROOM
4 STUDENT LOCKERS
5 STUDENT COMMONS
6 VESTIBULE
7 OFFICE
18 ACADEMIC DEAN'S OFFICE
19 PRE-FUNCTION GALLERY
20 CLASSROOM
22 HERITAGE HALL
25 BALCONY
29 CONFERENCE/CLASSROOM
31 ATTIC
32 MECHANICAL PENTHOUSE
35 COVERED PORCH
36 CORRIDOR

35TH STREET

EAST-WEST SECTION

OWNER
Georgetown Visitation
Preparatory School

DATA

Type of Facility
Preparatory school

Type of Construction
Reconstruction

Historic Status
Contributing structure in a
National Register Historic
District

Area of Building
47,000 GSF

Total Project Cost
$10.6 million

Status of Project
Completed August 1995

CREDITS

Architect of Record
KressCox Associates, P.C.
2909 M Street, N.W.
Washington, D.C. 20007

Structural Engineer
McMullan and Associates
Vienna, Virginia

Mechanical/Electrical Engineer
Girard Engineering
McLean, Virginia

Lighting Consultant
Light 'N' Up
Washington, D.C.

Audiovisual Consultant
Miller/Henning
McLean, Virginia

Construction Manager
Whiting-Turner Contracting
Company
Bethesda, Maryland

Photographer
Maxwell Mackenzie
Washington, D.C.

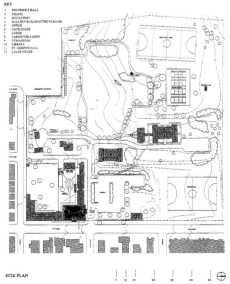

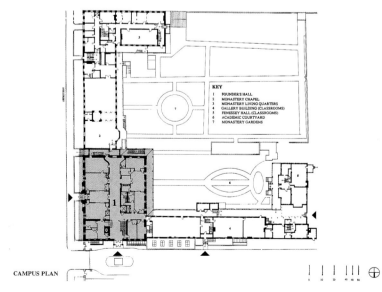

Whig and Clio Halls, Princeton University

Princeton, New Jersey

Ford Farewell Mills & Gatsch, Architects

ARCHITECT'S STATEMENT

Whig and Clio halls, designed in 1893, are Greek Revival structures clad in Vermont Danby marble. A century of weathering caused extensive cracking of the column bases and plinths and many other materials problems. Based on the evaluation of the buildings, the architectural team recommended replacing the column bases and plinths and reconstructing the column foundations. However, it was important to retain the monolithic columns, which can no longer be quarried in 22-foot-long blocks. Therefore, the team developed a unique clamping system to suspend the stone columns in place while their bases and plinths were removed and replaced with new material. In addition, the marble facades were cleaned, repointed, and repaired with newly carved marble dutchmen.

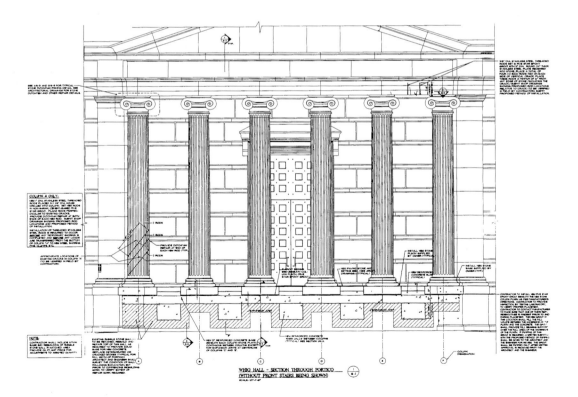

WHIG HALL – SECTION THROUGH PORTICO
(WITHOUT FRONT STAIRS BEING SHOWN)

OWNER
Princeton University

DATA
Type of Facility
University

Type of Construction
Special project

Historic Status
National Register of Historic
Places

Total Project Cost
$1.8 million

Status of Project
Completed November 1995

CREDITS
Architect of Record
Ford Farewell Mills & Gatsch,
Architects
864 Mapleton Road
Princeton, New Jersey 08540

Structural Engineer
Robert Silman Associates
New York, New York

Stone Consultant
Ivan Myjer
Society for the Preservation of
New England Antiquities
Waltham, Massachusetts

Conservator Consultant
George S. Wheeler
Metropolitan Museum of Art,
Objects Conservation
New York, New York

Sculptor
Nick Micros
New York, New York

Contractor
Lorenzon Brothers Company
Philadelphia, Pennsylvania

Contractor's Structural Engineer
Joseph B. Callaghan, Inc.
Consulting Engineers
Philadelphia, Pennsylvania

Photographers
Catherine Sellers
Princeton, New Jersey

Taylor Photo
Princeton, New Jersey

Building 01-020, Stanford University

Stanford, California

Page & Turnbull, Inc.

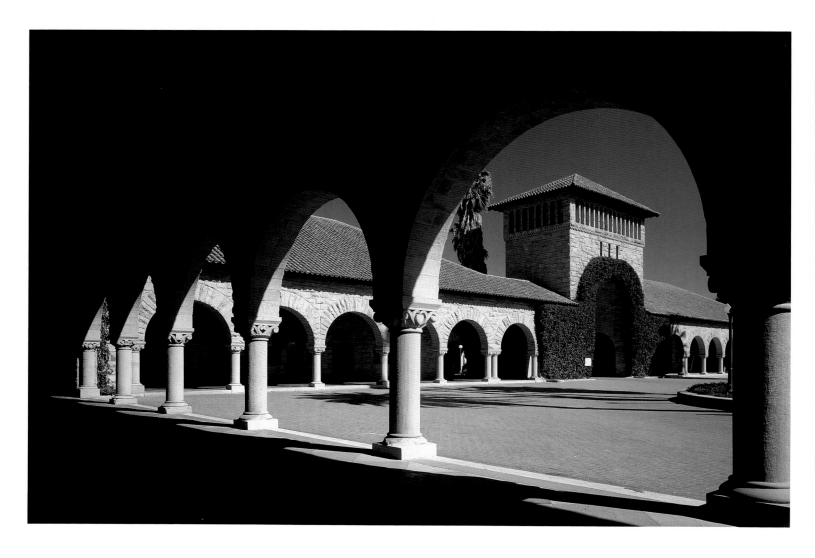

ARCHITECT'S STATEMENT

The 1989 Loma Prieta earthquake caused considerable damage throughout Stanford's campus and added urgency to the ongoing strengthening of the original, unreinforced masonry buildings in the university's Main Quadrangle. The various structural solutions for strengthening these buildings can be plainly seen by walking around the Quad, and the techniques used portray the evolution of the preservation philosophy over the decades. The structural solution for Building 01-020 was selected from more than six alternative strategies and evolved from several solutions used over twenty years on other Quad buildings. Removal of whole stones, instead of cutting or drilling, permitted replacement after the insertion of reinforcement and shotcrete. This method protected the visual integrity of the building from the potentially invasive strengthening process, and minimal historic material was lost.

OWNER
Stanford University

DATA

Type of Facility
University

Type of Construction
Rehabilitation

Historic Status
Eligible for the National
Register of Historic Places

Area of Building
10,000 GSF

Total Project Cost
$1.4 million

Status of Project
Completed April 1995

CREDITS

Architect of Record
Page & Turnbull, Inc.
724 Pine Street
San Francisco, California
94108

Structural Engineer
Degenkolb Engineers
San Francisco, California

Mechanical/Electrical Engineer
Flack & Kurtz—Consulting
Engineers, LLP
San Francisco, California

Project Cost Estimator
Adamson Associates
San Francisco, California

Contractor
Dinwiddie Construction
Company
San Francisco, California

Photographer
Alan Geller
San Francisco, California

SEISMIC STRENGTHENING

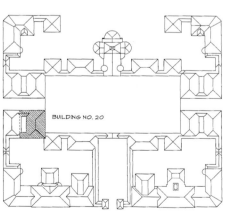

BUILDING NO. 20

SITE PLAN
MAIN QUADRANGLE

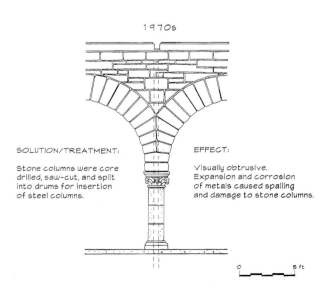

1970s

SOLUTION/TREATMENT:

Stone columns were core
drilled, saw-cut, and split
into drums for insertion
of steel columns.

EFFECT:

Visually obtrusive.
Expansion and corrosion
of metals caused spalling
and damage to stone columns.

0   5 ft

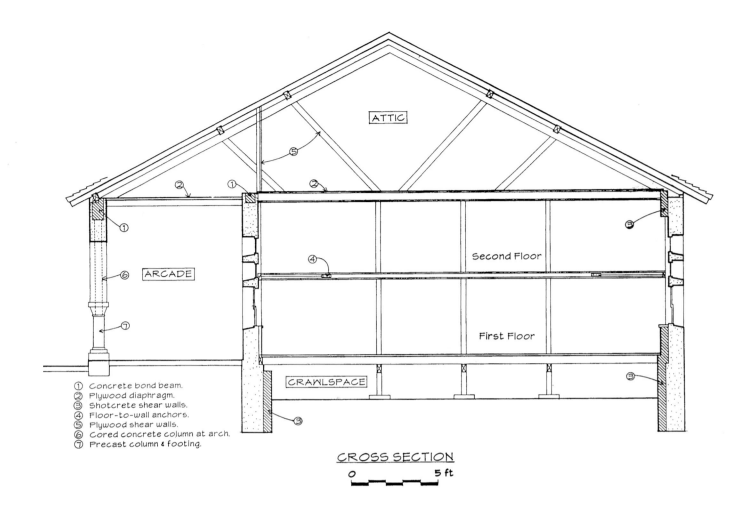

ATTIC

ARCADE

Second Floor

First Floor

CRAWLSPACE

① Concrete bond beam.
② Plywood diaphragm.
③ Shotcrete shear walls.
④ Floor-to-wall anchors.
⑤ Plywood shear walls.
⑥ Cored concrete column at arch.
⑦ Precast column & footing.

CROSS SECTION

0   5 ft

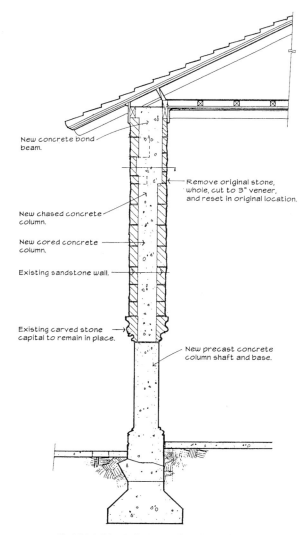

New concrete bond
beam.

New chased concrete
column.

New cored concrete
column.

Existing sandstone wall.

Existing carved stone
capital to remain in place.

Remove original stone,
whole, cut to 3" veneer,
and reset in original location.

New precast concrete
column shaft and base.

TYPICAL ARCADE SECTION

0   5 ft

University of Michigan Law School
Ann Arbor, Michigan

Quinn Evans/Architects

ARCHITECT'S STATEMENT

The main classroom building was one of the last to be built in the English Gothic-style law school complex. The interior treatment of the classrooms was inconsistent with the character of the rest of the buildings. Planning for a major building system upgrade offered the opportunity for a comprehensive treatment that emulates the richness and warmth found elsewhere in the complex. The most significant change was the addition of a distinctive design of ceiling coffers, ornamental plaster, decorative millwork, and custom-designed lighting fixtures to conceal mechanical ductwork.

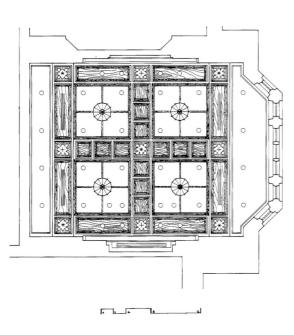

REFLECTED CEILING PLAN
ROOM 132

OWNER
University of Michigan

DATA

Type of Facility
University classrooms

Type of Construction
Rehabilitation

Historic Status
Contributing structure in a National Register Historic District

Area of Building
5,300 GSF

Total Project Cost
$1.1 million

Status of Project
Completed December 1994

CREDITS

Architect of Record
Quinn Evans/Architects
219 ½ North Main Street
Ann Arbor, Michigan 48104

Structural Engineer
Robert Darvas Associates
Ann Arbor, Michigan

Mechanical/Electrical Engineer
TMP Associates
Bloomfield Hills, Michigan

Interior Designer
University of Michigan Interiors
Ann Arbor, Michigan

Lighting Consultant
Gary Steffy Lighting Design, Inc.
Ann Arbor, Michigan

Contractor
J. C. Beal Construction, Inc.
Ann Arbor, Michigan

Photographer
Fred Golden
Ann Arbor, Michigan

Center for Southwest Research/Zimmerman General Library, University of New Mexico

Albuquerque, New Mexico

Van H. Gilbert Architect, P.C.

ARCHITECT'S STATEMENT

The challenge for this library addition, restoration, and renovation was designing the project in the context of the 1936 John Gaw Meem original Pueblo Revival architecture style. A 1960s glass entry addition to the library was replaced with an addition that is seamlessly linked to Meem's original building, strongly anchoring the library as the center-stone of this distinctively regional campus. The style and massing of the original 1936 building were incorporated in the design of the new building portions through the use of battered walls, stepped massing, traditional portals with corbeled columns at the entries, and deep-set windows with exposed lintels. These traditional design elements were expressed using contemporary materials.

At every level of planning and design this building responds to the indigenous style and climatic demands of its southwestern location, with features to provide shelter from the sun and control its heating effect through the use of overhangs and exterior shading devices.

Area of Building
76,400 GSF (rehabilitation)
33,500 GSF (new construction)

Total Project Cost
$6.3 million

Status of Project
Completed July 1993

CREDITS
Architect of Record/Interiors
Van H. Gilbert Architect, P.C.
319 Central Avenue, N.W.,
Suite 201
Albuquerque, New Mexico
87102

Associate Architect
Shepley Bulfinch Richardson &
Abbott
40 Broad Street
Boston, Massachusetts 02109

Structural Engineer
Randy Holt & Associates
Albuquerque, New Mexico

Mechanical Engineer
Bridgers & Paxton Consulting
Engineers
Albuquerque, New Mexico

Electrical Engineer
Telcon Engineering, Inc.
Albuquerque, New Mexico

Interior Lighting
Grenald & Associates
Narberth, Pennsylvania

Landscape Architect
G. Robert Johns, ASLA
Albuquerque, New Mexico

Contractor
Jaynes Corporation
Albuquerque, New Mexico

Photographer
Alexander Vertikoff
Venice, California

OWNER
University of New Mexico

DATA
Type of Facility
University

Type of Construction
Rehabilitation and new construction

Historic Status
Eligible for the National Register
of Historic Places

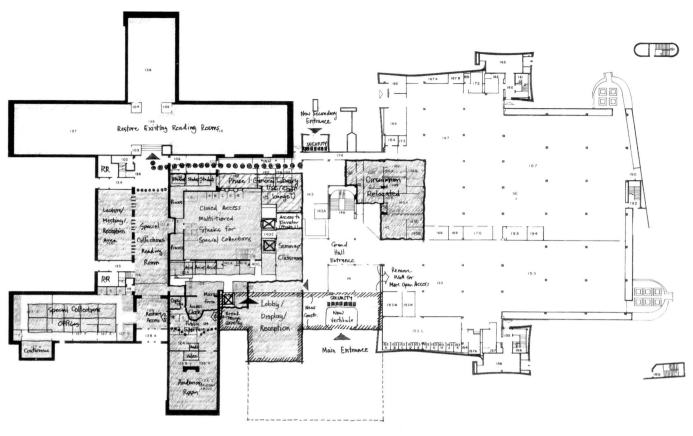

GROUND LEVEL FLOOR PLAN   ZIMMERMAN LIBRARY – CENTER FOR SOUTHWEST RESEARCH

Gunter Hall, University of Northern Colorado

Greeley, Colorado

C. W. Fentress, J. H. Bradburn and Associates

ARCHITECT'S STATEMENT

Gunter Hall is the architectural symbol for the University of Northern Colorado. The challenge was to increase usable space within the building without affecting its primary historic character. The design solution was to insert an addition into the main gymnasium, designing around a central atrium to maintain the original light and airy character. The collegiate Gothic windows, brick and terra-cotta facades, ornamental plaster, millwork, light fixtures, mechanical grilles, and interior finishes were restored. Environmentally appropriate features and materials include natural ventilation, daylighting, and off-gassing prior to occupancy.

Area of Building
92,000 GSF

Total Project Cost
$8.575 million

Status of Project
Phase I completed December 1995

Phase II completed August 1996

CREDITS

Architect of Record
C. W. Fentress, J. H. Bradburn and Associates
421 Broadway
Denver, Colorado 80203

Structural Engineer
Martin/Martin, Inc.
Wheat Ridge, Colorado

Mechanical/Electrical Engineer
Engineering Economics, Inc.
Denver, Colorado

Acoustical and Audiovisual Consultant
David L. Adams Associates, Inc.
Denver, Colorado

Environmental Consultant
Richard L. Crowther, FAIA
Denver, Colorado

Cost Estimating Consultant
Architectural Resource Consultants, Inc.
Boulder, Colorado

Smoke Management Consultant
Dillon Consulting Engineers, Inc.
Long Beach, California

Peer Review Consultant
Riegel Associates, Inc.
Englewood, Colorado

Contractor
Rhoads Construction Company, Inc.
Fort Collins, Colorado

Photographer
Ron Johnson
Johnson Associates
Denver, Colorado

OWNER
University of Northern Colorado

DATA

Type of Facility
University

Type of Construction
Restoration, rehabilitation, and special project

Historic Status
Eligible for the National Register of Historic Places

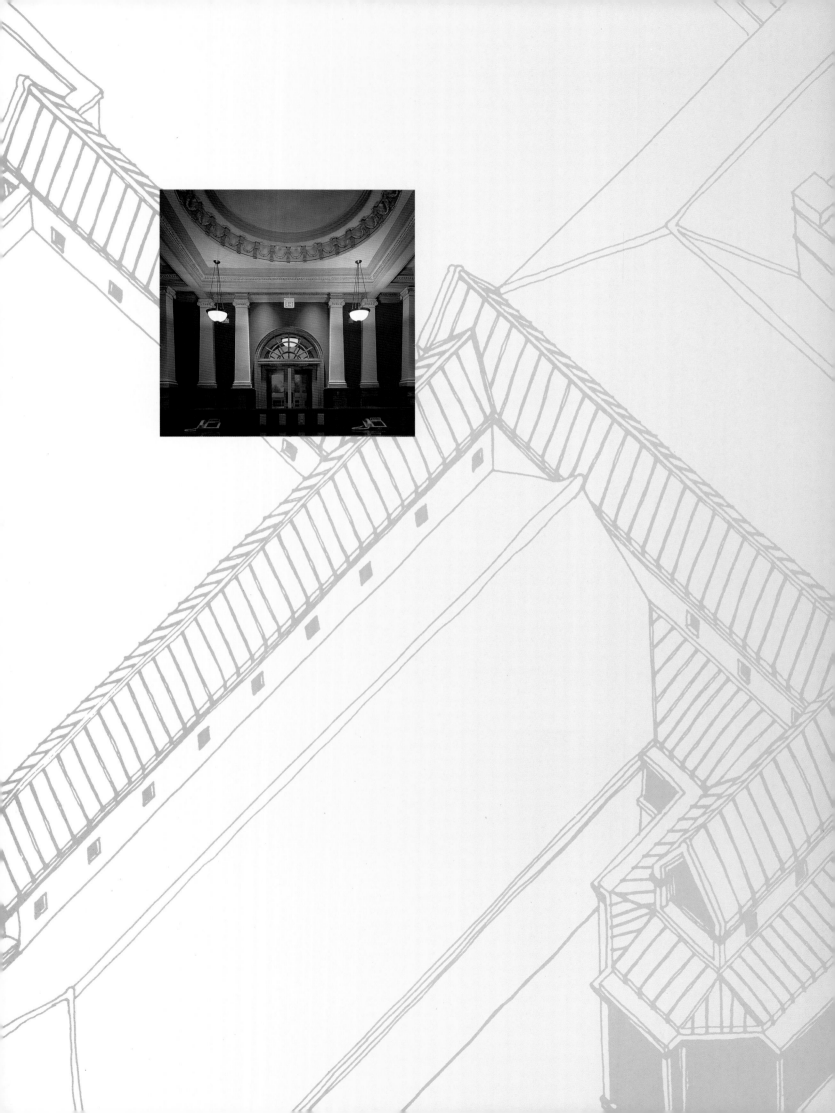

Libraries

A. K. Smiley Library

Redlands, California

Architectural Resources Group, Architects, Planners, & Conservators, Inc.

The challenge was to expand an existing historic building constructed in 1898, in a tight site, while retaining the park-like setting. The architect prepared a master plan for the expansion that included programming for the facility, a detailed phasing plan to allow the library to remain open during expansion, and construction documents.

The addition is configured in two wings, each with a single story and a basement. The wings house adult services, historical and rare books, a children's room, and support services. The design and materials are in harmony with the older structure. Existing interior spaces were redesigned to function more efficiently. Landscape plans include two formal gardens between the new and old wings. All plans were subject to review by the State Office of Historic Preservation and met the U.S. Secretary of the Interior's *Standards for Rehabilitation*.

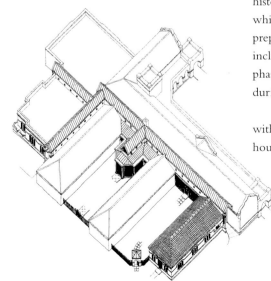

ISOMETRIC

OWNER
   City of Redlands

DATA
   Type of Facility
   Public library

   Type of Construction
   Rehabilitation

   Historic Status
   National Register of Historic
   Places
   State and local landmark

   Area of Buildings
   33,000 GSF (existing)
   10,000 GSF (addition

   Total Project Cost
   $3.5 million

   Status of Project
   Completed October 1990

CREDITS
   Architect of Record
   Architectural Resources Group,
   Architects, Planners, &
   Conservators, Inc.
   Pier 9
   The Embarcadero
   San Francisco, California
   94111

   Structural Engineer
   Johnson & Neilsen Associates
   Riverside, California

   Mechanical/Electrical Engineer
   TMAD Engineers, Inc.
   San Bernadino, California

   Cost Estimator
   Adamson Associates
   Santa Monica, California

   Landscape Architect
   Emmet L. Wemple &
   Associates Landscape
   Architects
   Los Angeles, California

   Contractor
   DMH, Inc., Contractors
   Redlands, California

   Photographer
   Mike Blumensaadt
   San Francisco, California

Center for Motion Picture Study
Beverly Hills, California

Offenhauser/Mekeel Architects

ARCHITECT'S STATEMENT

It was a Hollywood rags-to-riches story—transforming an abandoned water-treatment plant into the nation's premier library and archive of print materials about film. The Spanish Revival building was restored on the outside—with window reconstruction, concrete-epoxy injection, and ornament recasting. A new wing was added in a compatible style. Inside, the raw concrete shell with its huge sand beds and pipes was transformed. The architects retained the unique shapes of the aerator, tanks, and other industrial spaces by deftly concealing new shear walls, elevators, stairs, sprinklers, conduits, and ductwork. Virtually no new walls or suspended ceilings were added. Birch and cherry woodwork defines the library's new spaces.

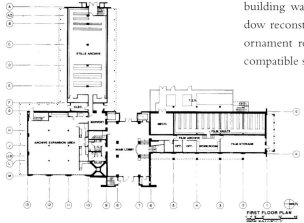

OWNER
　Academy of Motion Picture Arts
　and Sciences

DATA
Type of Facility
　Library and archive

Type of Construction
　Rehabilitation

Historic Status
　Eligible for the National
　Register of Historic Places

Area of Building
　40,000 GSF

Total Project Cost
　$7 million

Status of Project
　Completed January 1991

CREDITS
Design Architect
　Offenhauser/Mekeel Architects
　8762 Holloway Drive
　West Hollywood, California
　90069

Executive Architect
　Leidenfrost/Horowitz &
　Associates
　1833 South Victory Boulevard
　Glendale, California 91201

Structural Engineer
　Grossman and Speer
　Associates
　Glendale, California

Mechanical Engineer
　Rosenberg & Associates
　Los Angeles, California

Electrical Engineer
　Calpec Engineering
　Pasadena, California

Construction Management
　Gerald McKenna
　Culver City, California

Contractor
　Illig Construction
　Los Angeles, California

Photographer
　Nick Springett
　Beverly Hills, California

Howell Carnegie Library

Howell, Michigan

David W. Osler Associates (formerly Osler/Milling Architects) and Quinn Evans/Architects

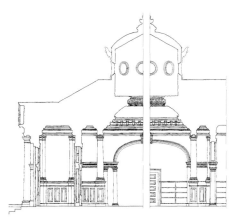

INTERIOR SECTION AT ROTUNDA

ARCHITECT'S STATEMENT

The Howell Carnegie Library was designed in 1903 by Elijah E. Meyers, the architect of the Michigan State Capitol. The strict classical plan and the detailing are typical of Carnegie libraries of this period. The client proposed the renovation of the existing structure and the construction of an addition without compromising the existing structure's architectural character.

Interior restoration involved extensive reconstruction of decorative plaster, architectural woodwork, and decorative painting. Exterior restoration involved cleaning and repairing the stonework, and interfacing a new standing-seam metal roof with existing decorative metal cornices, pediments, and cupola cladding.

OWNER
Howell Carnegie District Library

DATA

Type of Facility
Public library

Type of Construction
Restoration

Historic Status
National Register of Historic Places

Area of Buildings
7,000 GSF (existing)
23,000 GSF (addition)

Total Project Cost
$5 million

Status of Project
Completed March 1991

CREDITS

Architect of Record
David W. Osler Associates
(formerly Osler/Milling Architects)
916 Fuller Road
Ann Arbor, Michigan 48104

Restoration Architect
Quinn Evans/Architects
219 ½ North Main Street
Ann Arbor, Michigan 48104

Structural Engineer
Robert Darvas Associates
Ann Arbor, Michigan

Mechanical Engineer
Professional Consultants, Inc.
Livonia, Michigan

Electrical Engineer
Bada Engineering, Inc.
Livonia, Michigan

Lighting Designer
Gary Steffy Lighting Design, Inc.
Ann Arbor, Michigan

Interior Designer
Riemenschneider Design, Inc.
Ann Arbor, Michigan

Landscape Architect
John Grissim & Associates
Farmington Hills, Michigan

Contractor
The Christman Company
Flint, Michigan

Photographer
Fred Golden
Ann Arbor, Michigan

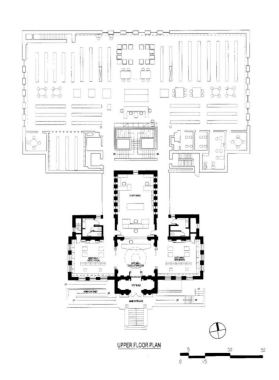

UPPER FLOOR PLAN

Nantucket Atheneum

Nantucket, Massachusetts

Ann Beha Associates, Inc.

ARCHITECT'S STATEMENT

This 1847 Greek Revival landmark serves as the public library and cultural center for a year-round community of 6,000 and a summer population of 40,000. The renovation provided expanded, state-of-the-art library services while preserving the historic features. Work included excavation to create additional space under the building and minimize impact on the adjacent park; restoration of the second-floor Great Hall for a research center; relocation of the children's collections from a damp basement to a new wing designed to meet stringent design-review requirements; and relandscaping of the surrounding park.

Section through Great Hall and Children's wing.

OWNER
Nantucket Atheneum

DATA

Type of Facility
Library

Type of Construction
Rehabilitation and expansion

Historic Status
Contributing structure in a
National Register Historic
District

Area of Building
13,000 GSF

Total Project Cost
$2.3 million

Status of Project
Completed April 1996

CREDITS

Architect of Record
Ann Beha Associates, Inc.
33 Kingston Street
Boston, Massachusetts 02111

Structural Engineer
Ocmulgee Associates
Ipswich, Massachusetts

Mechanical/Electrical Engineer
Architectural Engineers, Inc.
Boston, Massachusetts

Library Consultant
Rodney Armstrong
Boston, Massachusetts

Lighting Consultant
Ripman Lighting
Boston, Massachusetts

Landscape Architect
Smith & Co.
Boston, Massachusetts

Contractor
J. K. Scanlan Company, Inc.
West Bridgewater,
Massachusetts

Photographer
Hewitt-Garrison Architectural
Photographers
San Diego, California

Parlin Memorial Library
Everett, Massachusetts

CBT/Childs Bertman Tseckares, Inc.

ARCHITECT'S STATEMENT

This project involved complete renovation and major additions to an existing Romanesque Revival library. The primary goal of the project was to create a modern, revitalized library that would meet future community needs while retaining the historic character of the existing building. The form, scale, and decorative expression of the addition relate to the older building. Interior spaces are organized around a simple circulation spine that links one end of the building with the other, making it easier to find one's way in the library.

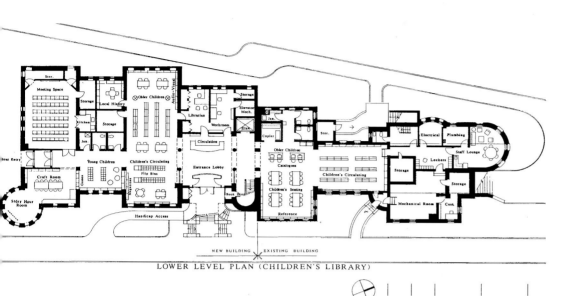

NEW BUILDING | EXISTING BUILDING

LOWER LEVEL PLAN (CHILDREN'S LIBRARY)

0   10'   20'   40'   60'

OWNER
City of Everett

DATA
Type of Facility
Public library

Type of Construction
Restoration and expansion

Historic Status
State landmark

Area of Building
20,000 GSF

Total Project Cost
$3.2 million

Status of Project
Completed September 1992

CREDITS
Architect of Record
CBT/Childs Bertman
Tseckares, Inc.
306 Dartmouth Street
Boston, Massachusetts 02116

Structural Engineer
Aberjona Engineering
Winchester, Massachusetts

Mechanical/Electrical Engineer
Shooshanian Engineering
Associates
Boston, Massachusetts

Lighting Design
D. Schweppe Lighting
Concord, Massachusetts

Acoustical Engineer
Cambridge Acoustical
Engineers
Cambridge, Massachusetts

Contractor
Seaman Bratko Corporation
Boston, Massachusetts

Photographers
Steve Rosenthal
Auburndale, Massachusetts
Aaron Usher
Pawtucket, Rhode Island

Williams Research Center
New Orleans, Louisiana

Jahncke Architects, Inc.

ARCHITECT'S STATEMENT

The restoration and adaptive reuse of a dilapidated 1915 Edgar A. Christy Beaux Arts court building in the French Quarter resulted in a state-of-the-art library and archive. The expanded facility doubles the previous archive storage capacity of the Historic New Orleans Collection and provides a well-organized series of work spaces for archivists, curators, librarians, and researchers.

The building was transformed into a modern research institution within the historic exterior fabric, and the distinctive original interior elements were maintained. The exterior was returned to its original detailing while the interior was painstakingly restored using the scale and details from the existing building's Tuscan classical order.

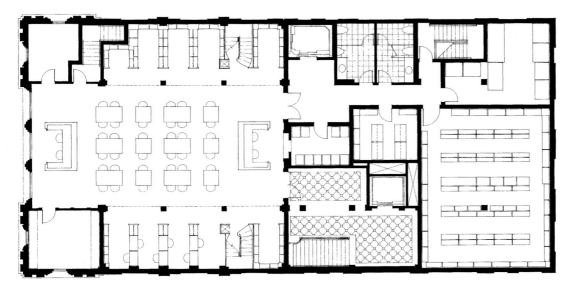

SECOND FLOOR PLAN 0 1'   5'   10'

OWNER
The Kemper & Leila Williams
Foundation

DATA
Type of Facility
Library and archive

Type of Construction
Restoration and adaptive reuse

Historic Status
Contributing structure in a
National Register Historic District
State and local landmark

Area of Building
14,400 GSF

Total Project Cost
$3.125 million

Status of Project
Completed January 1996

CREDITS
Architect of Record
Jahncke Architects, Inc.
3516 Magazine Street
New Orleans, Louisiana 70115

Structural Engineer
Jeffrey, Thomas, Avegno, Inc.
New Orleans, Louisiana

Mechanical Engineers
Warren G. Moses
New Orleans, Louisiana
Peter L. Hilbert
New Orleans, Louisiana

Electrical Engineers
Warren G. Moses
New Orleans, Louisiana
Marvin Electric
New Orleans, Louisiana

Shelving and Storage Systems
Associated Office Systems
of Louisiana
Metairie, Louisiana

Contractor
Carl E. Woodward
New Orleans, Louisiana

Photographer
Historic New Orleans Collection,
Jan White Brantley
New Orleans, Louisiana

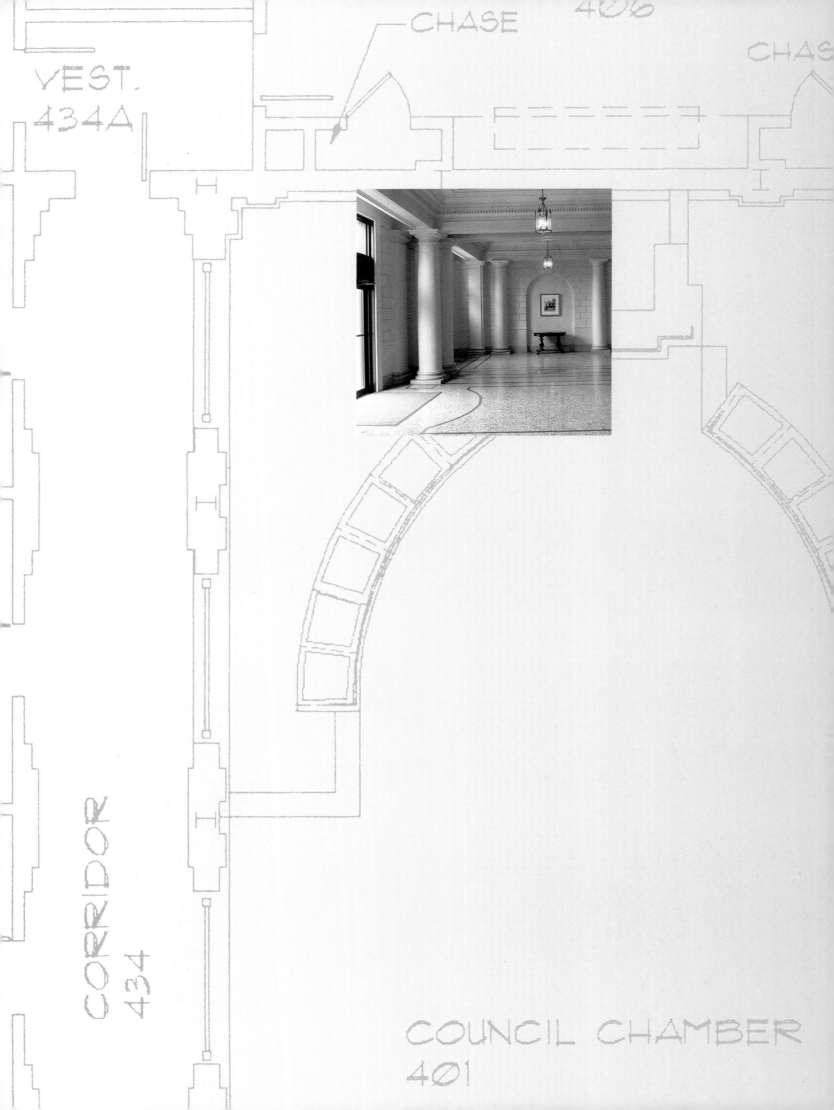

CHASE 406

CHASE

VEST.
434A

CORRIDOR
434

COUNCIL CHAMBER
401

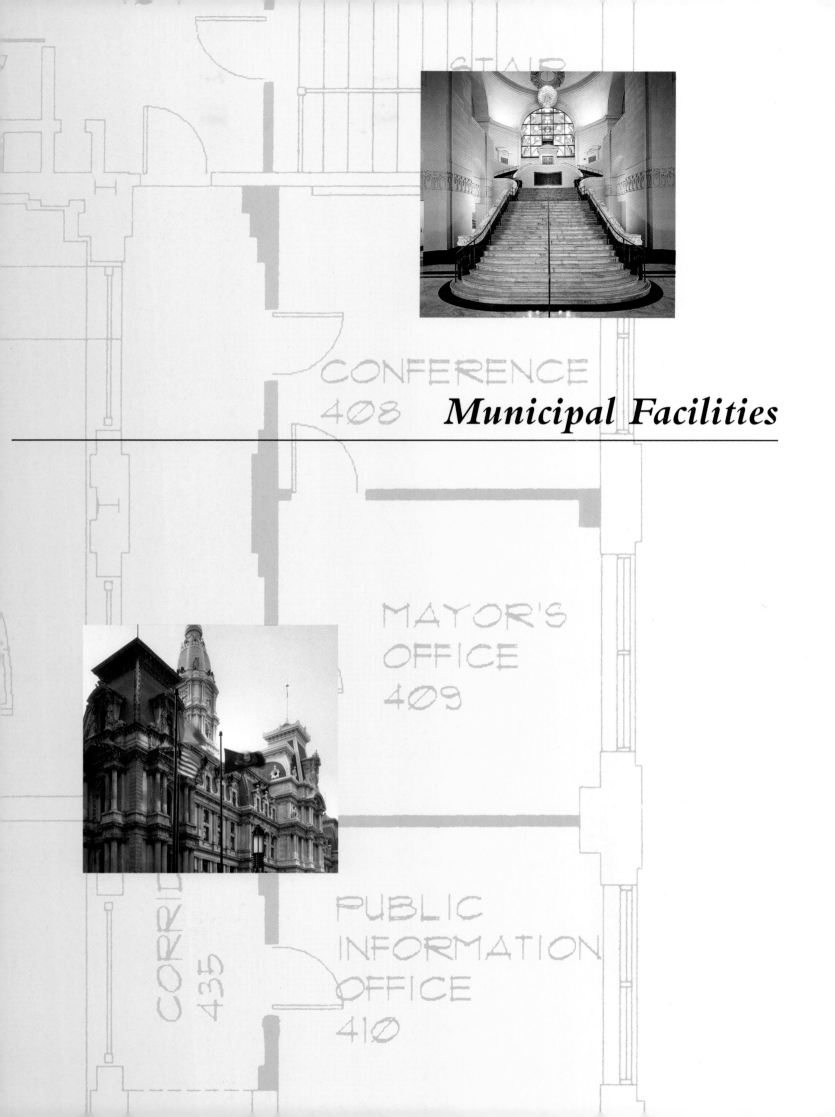

Municipal Facilities

Danville Municipal Building
Danville, Virginia

Dewberry & Davis and Joseph Dye Lahendro

ARCHITECT'S STATEMENT

Renovation work to this five-story building includes the removal of nonoriginal construction and the restoration of all spaces to their original condition to the greatest extent possible. The entire building will receive new plumbing, heating/ventilation/air-conditioning and electrical-communications systems and will be brought into compliance with current barrier-free access standards. Highlights of this project include restoration of the building's main lobby on the second floor and city council chambers on the fourth floor to their original appearance.

OWNER
City of Danville

DATA
Type of Facility
Municipal office building

Type of Construction
Restoration and rehabilitation

Historic Status
National Register of Historic Places
State landmark

Area of Building
70,000 GSF

Total Project Cost
$2.099 million

Status of Project
Phases I through IV completed March 1996

CREDITS
Architect of Record
Dewberry & Davis
551 Piney Forest Road
Danville, Virginia 24543

Historic Architect
Joseph Dye Lahendro
204 West Franklin Street
Richmond, Virginia 23220

Structural/Mechanical/Electrical Engineer
Dewberry & Davis
Raleigh, North Carolina

Acoustical/Sound System Consultant
Consulting for Theater Systems
Front Royal, Virginia

Interiors Consultant
Haynesworth's Office Products
Danville, Virginia

Contractor
Blair Construction
Gretna, Virginia

Photographer
Joseph Romeo Photography
Fairfax, Virginia

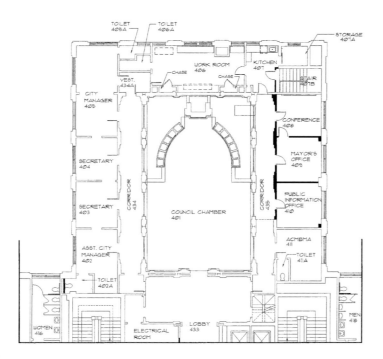

PARTIAL FOURTH FLOOR RENOVATION PLAN

Oakland City Hall

Oakland, California

VBN Architects and Carey & Company, Inc., Architecture

ARCHITECT'S STATEMENT

Oakland City Hall, listed in the National Register of Historic Places, was the first Beaux Arts high-rise municipal office building in the country. Since it was critically damaged in the 1989 Loma Prieta earthquake, this structure has become the first existing high-rise building in the world to be fitted with base isolators, the giant rubber shock absorbers that dissipate seismic energy.

The city hall's public gathering and ceremonial spaces were completely restored during the project. Modern telecommunication and broadcast technology was carefully integrated into the city council chambers. The mayor's office was restored to its original appearance with features re-created from original drawings found in city archives. Four skylights on the third floor that had been covered for at least fifty years were reopened and renovated. The elaborate clock tower was completely restored, as were the original stone finishes, terra-cotta, plaster, fine woodwork, and ornamental lighting fixtures.

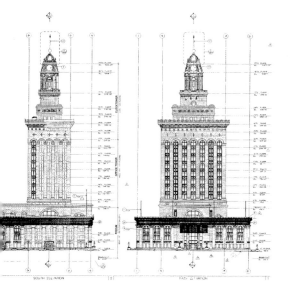

OWNER
City of Oakland

DATA
Type of Facility
City hall

Type of Construction
Rehabilitation

Historic Status
National Register of Historic Places

Area of Building
153,000 GSF

Total Project Cost
$63.1 million

Status of Project
Completed September 1995

CREDITS
Architect
VBN Architects
501 14th Street, Suite 300
Oakland, California 94612

Associated Architect
Michael Willis & Associates, Architects
246 First Street, Suite 200
San Francisco, California 94105

Preservation Architect
Carey & Company, Inc., Architecture
123 Townsend Street, Suite 400
San Francisco, California 94107

Structural Engineer
Forell/Elsesser Engineers, Inc.
San Francisco, California

Mechanical Engineer
SJ Engineers
Oakland, California

Electrical Engineer
Silverman & Light
Emeryville, California

Construction Manager
Turner Construction
San Francisco, California

Photographer
Vittoria Visuals
San Francisco, California

Philadelphia City Hall
Philadelphia, Pennsylvania

Vitetta Group

ARCHITECT'S STATEMENT

Among the world's largest and tallest historic masonry structures, this National Historic Landmark is the focus of a series of multimillion-dollar restoration projects by the city planned for the next ten years. After a national search in 1991, the architectural/engineering team was selected by the city for comprehensive planning services. The four-year planning and research effort led to a plan that is intended to reverse decades of deferred maintenance and inappropriate alterations by comprehensively addressing the building's history, existing conditions, planned uses, restoration, and maintenance. Current restoration work includes life-safety improvements throughout the building, new public toilet facilities and stairs, and the restoration of exterior facades (marble, granite, and mahogany windows) and cast-iron work.

Historic Status
National Historic Landmark

Area of Building
1,200,000 GSF

Total Project Cost
$54.8 million

Status of Project
Phase I estimated completion date: 1999

CREDITS

Architect of Record/ Mechanical/Electrical Engineer
Vitetta Group
The Wallace Building
642 North Broad Street
Philadelphia, Pennsylvania
19130

Associate Architect
Kelly/Maiello, Inc., Architects and Planners
37 South 20th Street
Philadelphia, Pennsylvania
19130

Structural Engineer
Keast & Hood
Philadelphia, Pennsylvania

Consulting Architects
Marianna Thomas Architects
Philadelphia, Pennsylvania
John Milner Architects, Inc.
Chadds Ford, Pennsylvania

Acoustics Consultant
Cerami & Associates, Inc.
New York, New York

Code-Analysis Consultant
Schirmer Engineering Corporation
Falls Church, Virginia

Cost-Estimating and Hazardous Materials Consultant
Hill International, Inc.
Willingboro, New Jersey

Cost-Estimating and Scheduling Consultant
Arena & Company
Wallingford, Pennsylvania

Graphic Designer
Cloud & Gershan Associates, Inc.
Philadelphia, Pennsylvania

Imagineer Consultant
Halcyon/Ernst & Young
Washington, D.C.

Landscape Architect
Menke & Menke
Swarthmore, Pennsylvania

Paint-Analysis Consultant
Frank S. Welsh Company
Bryn Mawr, Pennsylvania

Interior Designer
Interior Environment, Inc.
Philadelphia, Pennsylvania

Lighting Designer
Grenald Waldron & Associates
Narberth, Pennsylvania

Fine Arts Conservation Consultant
Norton Art Conservation, Inc.
Lafayette Hill, Pennsylvania

Communication Consultant
DeLuca Everett & Company
North Brunswick, New Jersey

Elevators Consultant
Performance Profiles, Inc.
Merion Station, Pennsylvania

Programming Consultant
WRP Consultants
Wynnewood, Pennsylvania

Contractors
CAD Electric
Newtown Square, Pennsylvania
Daniel J. Keating Company
Ardmore, Pennsylvania
Schneider Restorations, Inc.
Newtown, Pennsylvania
W. S. Cumbey & Sons, Inc.
Swarthmore, Pennsylvania
RMC Electrical Contractors, Inc.
Morton, Pennsylvania
Neshaminy Constructors, Inc.
Feasterville, Pennsylvania
Schleig Electrical, Inc.
Churchville, Pennsylvania

Photographers
Tom Crane Photography
Bryn Mawr, Pennsylvania
Joanne Bening
Philadelphia, Pennsylvania
J. Kyle Keener
Philadelphia, Pennsylvania

OWNER
City of Philadelphia, Department of Public Property

DATA
Type of Facility
City hall

Type of Construction
Restoration

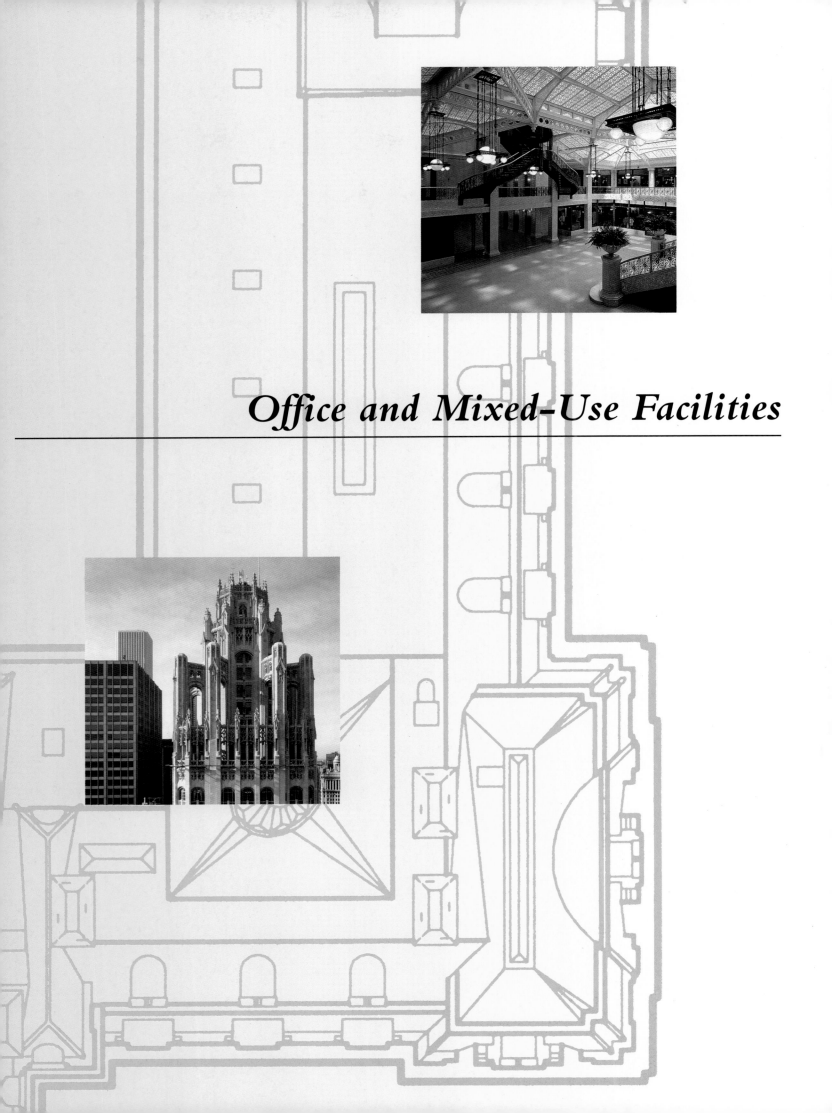

Office and Mixed-Use Facilities

Chicago Tribune Building

Chicago, Illinois

Wiss, Janney, Elstner Associates, Inc.

ARCHITECT'S STATEMENT

The Chicago Tribune Building, constructed in 1925, was the result of an internationally heralded competition. The Gothic skyscraper combines traditional materials, ornamental detailing, and the contemporary architectural form of the high-rise office building.

Careful analysis of the facade revealed that the limestone was in good condition, but the metal support systems were corroding. The facade renovation and cleaning program was developed using state-of-the-art analyses, traditional restoration techniques, and durable materials. A high standard of sensitivity was adopted in the conservation of all carved stonework. The project was closely monitored by the National Park Service for compliance with the U.S. Secretary of the Interior's *Standards for Rehabilitation*.

OWNER
Chicago Tribune Company

DATA

Type of Facility
Commercial offices

Type of Construction
Special project

Historic Status
Contributing structure in a
National Register Historic District

Area of Building
525,000 GSF

Total Project Cost
Not available

Status of Project
Completed October 1995

CREDITS

Architect of Record/Structural Engineer
Wiss, Janney, Elstner
Associates, Inc.
29 North Wacker Drive,
Suite 555
Chicago, Illinois 60606

Masonry Contractor
L. Page Corporation
Bellwood, Illinois

Facade-Cleaning Contractor
Thomann-Hanry
Paris, France

Photographer
Leslie Schwartz
Chicago, Illinois

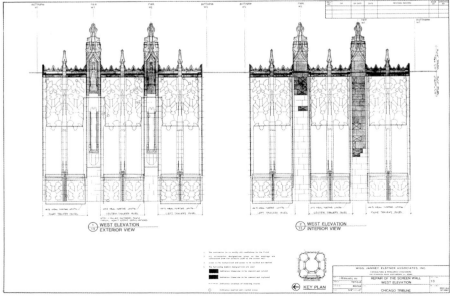

Greyhound Building

Washington, D.C.

Keyes Condon Florance Architects and Vitetta Group/Studio Four

ARCHITECT'S STATEMENt

Opened in 1940, Greyhound's then super-modern facility became obscured by later modernization that covered up all surfaces except the original floor. When the Greyhound station was closed in 1987, public sentiment ran high against demolition or mere facade restoration. The architectural/engineering team hired to restore the terminal and develop plans for an adjacent office building worked with local preservationists to preserve the terminal and make the project feasible. A pivotal design decision was to use the historic terminal as the main entrance for the new twelve-story office building to be built directly behind it. Plans and details were reviewed for compatibility with the original streamlined Art Deco details.

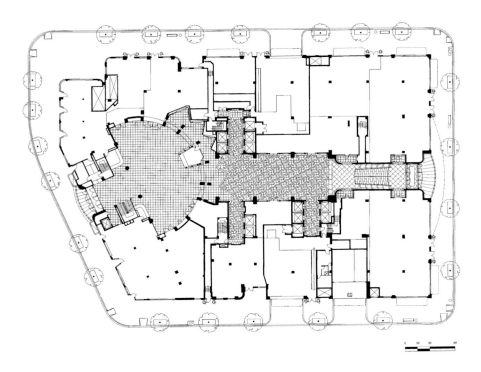

OWNER
  Manulife Real Estate

DATA
  Type of Facility
  Office building

  Type of Construction
  Restoration

  Historic Status
  Eligible for the National Register
  of Historic Places
  Local landmark

  Area of Building
  690,000 GSF

  Total Project Cost
  $45 million

  Status of Project
  Completed December 1991

CREDITS
  Architect of Record
  Keyes Condon Florance Architects
  1100 New York Avenue, NW
  Washington, D.C. 20005

  Restoration Architect
  Vitetta Group/Studio Four
  642 North Broad Street
  Philadelphia, Pennsylvania 19130

  Structural Engineer
  Tadjer-Cohen-Edelson Associates
  Silver Spring, Maryland

  Mechanical/Electrical/Plumbing
  Engineer
  Shefferman & Bigelson Company
  Silver Spring, Maryland

  Civil Engineer
  Wiles Dailey Pronske
  Reston, Virginia

  Contractor
  A. S. McGaughan Company, Inc.
  Calverton, Maryland

  Photographers
  Michael Dersin
  Arlington, Virginia
  Carol Highsmith
  Washington, D.C.
  Doug Brown
  Arlington, Virginia

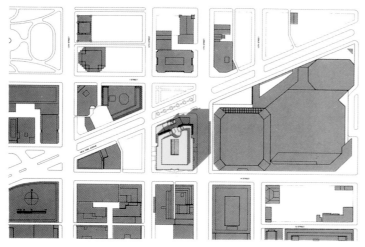

**Office and Mixed-Use
Facilities**

Old Executive Office Building

Washington, D.C.

Quinn Evans/Architects

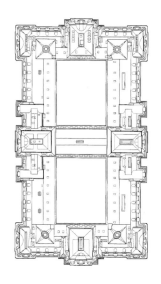

ROOF PLAN

ARCHITECT'S STATEMENT

Originally constructed in the late 1880s as the State, War, and Navy Building, the Old Executive Office Building is perhaps the best surviving example of Second Empire style architecture in the United States. In the early 1980s the General Services Administration began the ongoing preservation and revitalization of both the interior and exterior of the structure. Room 278, occupied by Theodore Roosevelt while he was Assistant Secretary of the Navy in 1897, was restored to its original character and grandeur in 1992. The restoration of the building's detailed granite upper facades and ornate mansard roof was completed in 1995.

OWNER
General Services
Administration

DATA
Type of Facility
Government office building

Type of Construction
Restoration

Historic Status
National Historic Landmark

Area of Project
100,000 SF (roof)

Total Project Cost
Not available

Status of Project
Completed March 1995

CREDITS
Architect
Quinn Evans/Architects
1214 28th Street, N.W.
Washington, D.C. 20007

Structural Engineer
FDE Ltd., Consulting Engineers
Alexandria, Virginia

Mechanical/Electrical Engineer
Smith & Faass Consulting
Engineers
Germantown, Maryland

Construction Manager
Sverdrup Facilities
Arlington, Virginia

Contractor
Charles H. Riddle Associates,
Inc./Roofers Inc.—Joint Venture
Kensington, Maryland

Conservator (Room 278)
Darla M. Olson
New York, New York

Photographer
Larry Olsen
Washington, D.C.

Pacific Gas & Electric Company
San Francisco, California

Kendall Heaton Associates and Page & Turnbull, Inc.

ARCHITECT'S STATEMENT

The seismic retrofit of the Pacific Gas & Electric Company required elaborate planning to maintain high quality in all construction methods, ensuring public safety in future earthquakes and upholding Federal standards. Using similar materials that would relate with the original brick and stucco finishes, the interior courtyard was stripped and replaced with a new shear wall system to strengthen the building. On the exterior terra-cotta facades, an innovative technique of introducing joints will prevent lateral deformation by allowing movement. These measures minimized the visual impact of retrofit activities on existing materials and preserved the unreinforced masonry and steel-frame infill systems.

Main Street Elevation

0 5' 15' 30' 50'

OWNER
Pacific Gas & Electric Company

DATA
Type of Facility
Office building

Type of Construction
Rehabilitation and seismic retrofit

Historic Status
National Register of Historic Places

Area of Building
650,000 GSF

Total Project Cost
$178 million

Status of Project
Completed October 1995

CREDITS
Architect of Record
Kendall Heaton Associates
3050 Post Oak Boulevard, Suite 1000
Houston, Texas 77056

Design Architect
Simon Martin-Vegue Winkelstein Moris
501 Second Street
San Francisco, California 94107

Historic Architect
Page & Turnbull, Inc.
724 Pine Street
San Francisco, California 94108

Structural Engineer
Forell/Elsesser Engineers, Inc.
San Francisco, California

Mechanical/Electrical Engineer
Flack & Kurtz—Consulting Engineers, LLP
San Francisco, California

Contractor
Dinwiddie Construction Company
San Francisco, California

Photographer
William Porter, Architectural and Commercial Photography
San Francisco, California

Office and Mixed-Use Facilities

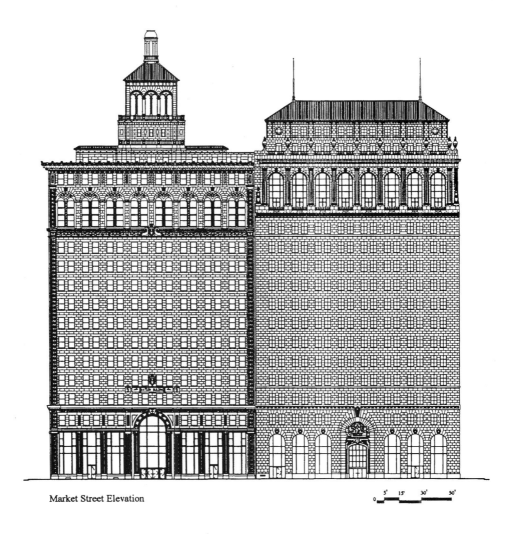

Market Street Elevation

0 5' 15' 30' 50'

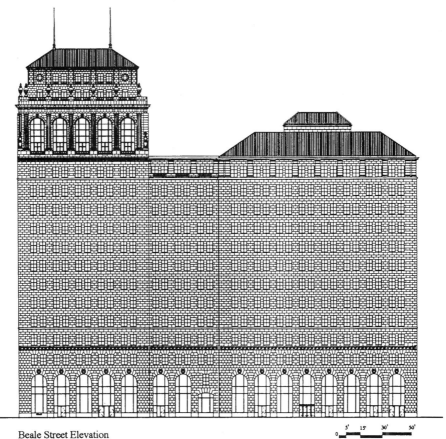

Beale Street Elevation

0 5' 15' 30' 50'

**Office and Mixed-Use
Facilities**

Postal Square

Washington, D.C.

Shalom Baranes Associates, P.C.

ARCHITECT'S STATEMENT

The Postal Square project involved the renovation and expansion of a landmarked city post office, designed by Daniel Burnham in 1912, for contemporary mixed use, including leasable office, retail, museum, and postal service uses. The building's most striking feature is its monumental Beaux Arts lobby, the grandeur of which was diminished by previous drastic alterations. Extant materials and photographic evidence were used to restore the lobby. An existing courtyard was infilled to create 400,000 square feet of new space with an atrium to bring daylight into interior offices. Attic areas were converted to additional office space. At ground level, a new retail postal facility was designed with a contemporary design derived from the historic interiors. All facades were cleaned and restored, new entrances and exits discreetly inserted, and state-of-the-art systems installed. The project houses the Smithsonian Postal Museum and facilities for several federal agencies.

CREDITS

Architect of Record
Shalom Baranes Associates, P.C.
3299 K Street, NW, Suite 400
Washington, D.C. 20007

Structural Engineer
KCE Structural Engineers
Washington, D.C.

Mechanical/Electrical Engineer
GHT, Chartered
Arlington, Virginia

Historic Preservation Consultant
Oehrlein & Associates
Washington, D.C.

Historic Finishes Consultant
Society for the Preservation of
New England Antiquities
Waltham, Massachusetts

*Historic and Architectural
Lighting Design*
Coventry Lighting Associates
Washington, D.C.

Landscape Architect
Stephenson and Good
Alexandria, Virginia

Historic Architectural Research
Traceries
Chevy Chase, Maryland

Contractor
A. S. McGaughan Company, Inc.
Calverton, Maryland

Photographers
Hedrich Blessing
Chicago, Illinois

Ronald N. Anderson,
Photographer
Rockville, Maryland

Alan Karchmer, Architectural
Photography
Washington, D.C.

OWNER
Postal Square Limited
Partnership

DATA

Type of Facility
Institutional, office, and retail

Type of Construction
Restoration and rehabilitation

Historic Status
Eligible for the National
Register of Historic Places
Local landmark

Area of Building
1,200,000 GSF

Total Project Cost
$150 million

Status of Project
Completed 1993

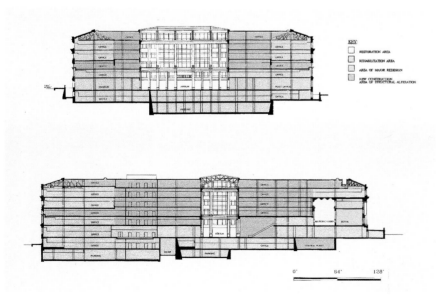

KEY:
RESTORATION AREA
REHABILITATION AREA
AREA OF MAJOR REDESIGN
NEW CONSTRUCTION
AREA OF STRUCTURAL ALTERATION

0'   64'   128'

The Rookery

Chicago, Illinois

McClier Corporation

ARCHITECT'S STATEMENT

Originally designed by the firm of Burnham & Root and completed in 1888, the Rookery was remodeled several times, first by Frank Lloyd Wright from 1905 to 1907, and then by William Drummond, circa 1930. Several other alterations were made during the next sixty years.

The design concept was to restore and reconstruct the most significant elements of this National Historic Landmark's three major periods and to combine them into a unified whole while incorporating all new mechanical/electrical/plumbing/fire-protection, security, and telecommunication systems that transformed it into a new, Class A office building.

OWNER
Baldwin Development Company

DATA

Type of Facility
Office and retail building

Type of Construction
Restoration and rehabilitation

Historic Status
National Historic Landmark
Local and state landmark

Area of Building
341,000 GSF

Total Project Cost
$110 million

Status of Project
Completed May 1992

CREDITS

Architect of Record/Restoration Architect
McClier Corporation
401 East Illinois, Suite 625
Chicago, Illinois 60611

Structural Engineer
Tylk, Gustafson and Associates
Chicago, Illinois

Mechanical/Electrical/Plumbing Engineer
Environmental Systems Design
Chicago, Illinois

Conservation Consultant
Hasbrouk, Peterson, Zimoch,
Sirirattamrong
Chicago, Illinois

Historic Finishes Consultant
Frank Matero
Graduate Program in Historic
Preservation
University of Pennsylvania
Philadelphia, Pennsylvania

Elevator Consultant
Edgett Williams Consulting Group, Inc.
Mill Valley, California

Contractor
Peck/Jones Construction Company
Chicago, Illinois

Photographer
Nick Merrick
Hedrich Blessing
Chicago, Illinois

**Office and Mixed-Use
Facilities**

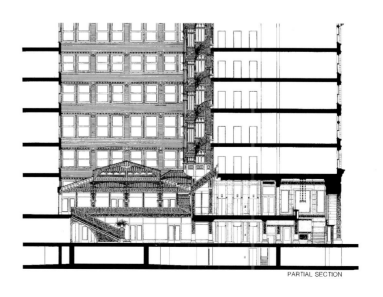

PARTIAL SECTION

**Office and Mixed-Use
Facilities**

Upper Pontalba Building
New Orleans, Louisiana

Sizeler Architects

ARCHITECT'S STATEMENT

The Upper Pontalba Building, built circa 1850, was designed by James Gallier and Henry Howard and inspired by the Palais Royal de Paris. The only major renovation was in 1930 by the Work Projects Administration. The objective of renovation was to identify and preserve the original design concepts while incorporating modern conveniences and life-safety features. The scope of services included new utilities, kitchens and bathrooms, central heating/ventilation/air-conditioning systems, partitions with wood base and cornices, flooring, finishes, a sprinkler system, fire/smoke-alarm detection, and emergency lighting. The original scale and aesthetic integrity of the structure were maintained: grand rooms with lofty ceilings; designs that were simply laid out and responsive to natural air flow and daylight; and door openings with wide wood trim, base, and cornice moldings.

OWNER
City of New Orleans, Upper Pontalba Building Restoration Corporation

DATA
Type of Facility
Apartment and commercial building

Type of Construction
Rehabilitation

Historic Status
National Register of Historic Places
Contributing structure in a National Register Historic District
State and local landmark

Area of Building
116,000 GSF

Total Project Cost
$6.7 million

Status of Project
Completed July 1995

CREDITS
Architect of Record
Sizeler Architects
300 Lafayette Street
Suite 200
New Orleans, Louisiana 70130

Structural Engineer
Schrenk & Peterson
New Orleans, Louisiana

Mechanical Engineer
Lace, Inc., Consulting Engineers
New Orleans, Louisiana

Electrical Engineer
IMC Consulting Engineers
Metairie, Louisiana

Contractor
Grimaldi Construction
New Orleans, Louisiana

Photographers
Thomas M. Brown, AIA
New Orleans, Louisiana
Neil Alexander
New Orleans, Louisiana

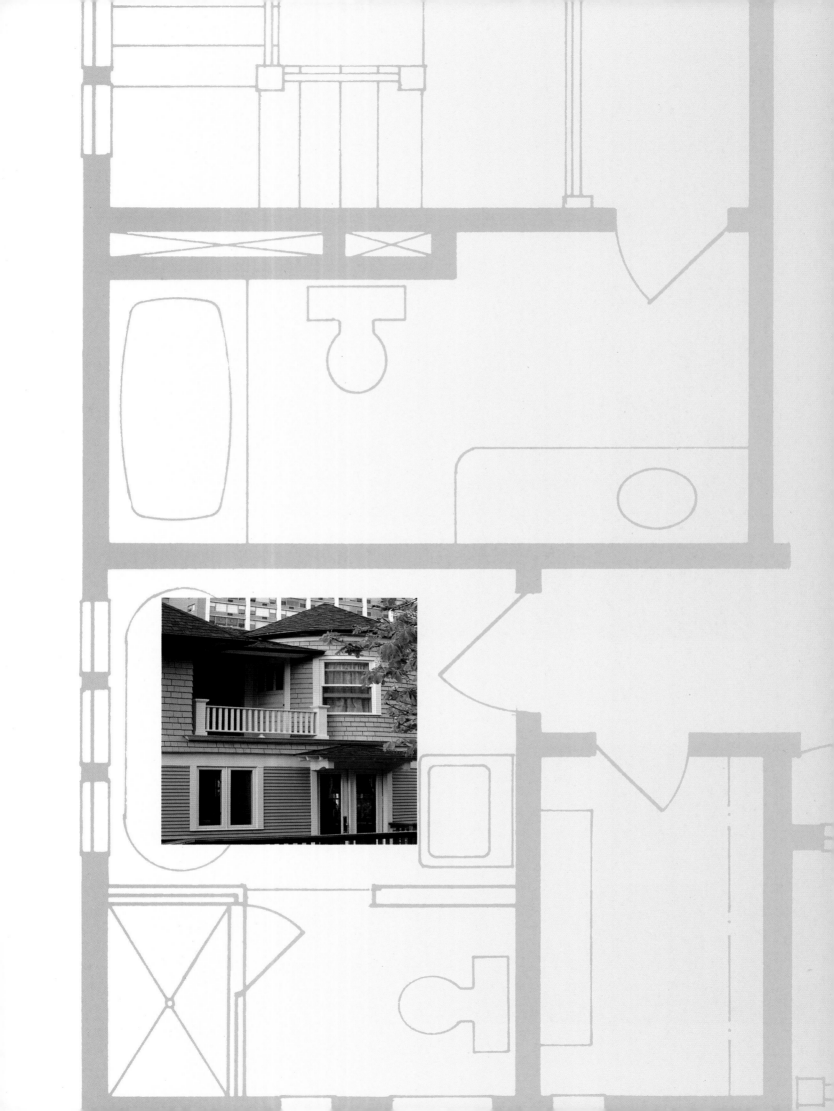

Residential Projects

Hutchinson Street Turret Addition

Chicago, Illinois

P. K. Vander Beke, Architect

ARCHITECT'S STATEMENT

A master bedroom suite was created by removing a roof and greenhouse addition and building a second story on top of the original porch, which previously had been converted into a kitchen. Using materials and details appropriate to this circa 1908 home in a landmark district, special care was taken to maintain appropriate scale and to be sensitive to the intent of the original design. The domed ceiling in the sitting room, wood wainscoting in the bathroom, and curved door leading to a small porch continue the tradition of fine craftwork found in the house.

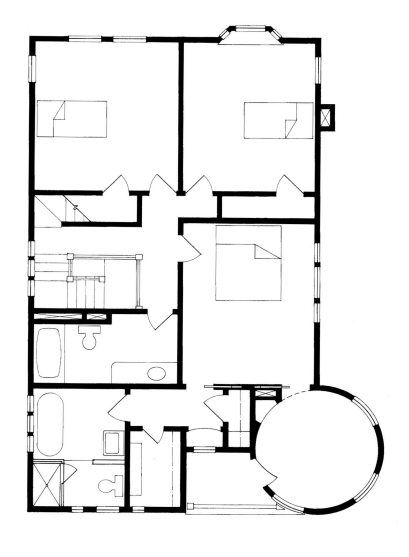

SECOND FLOOR PLAN
proposed

OWNERS
Howard and Ann Ferguson

DATA

Type of Facility
Residence

Type of Construction
Addition to historic structure

Historic Status
Local landmark

Area of Addition
384 GSF

Status of Project
Completed April 1994

CREDITS

Architect of Record
P. K. Vander Beke, Architect
505 North Lake Shore Drive
Chicago, Illinois 60611

Structural Engineer
James D. Senffner
Chicago, Illinois

Contractor
Bryan K. Henson
General Contractors, Inc.
Harvard, Illinois

Photographer
William Kildow Photography
Chicago, Illinois

Pennock Farmstead

Chester County, Pennsylvania

Susan Maxman Architects

ARCHITECT'S STATEMENT

Exemplifying the brick farmhouses built by Quakers in southeastern Pennsylvania during the late eighteenth and early nineteenth centuries, the essential qualities of this farmhouse are restraint, simple order, and utility. The original design integrity is extraordinary because of the absence of the turn-of-the-century modernization that is characteristic of many early structures in this region, and a thirty-year history of abandonment before 1990. The philosophy of the farmstead's renovation has been to conserve and preserve the details of the original design and material fabric while creating a house suitable for modern living.

DATA

Type of Facility
Residential

Type of Construction
Restoration

Historic Status
Eligible for the National
Register of Historic Places

Area of Building
5,500 GSF

Total Project Cost
Not available

Status of Project
Completed April 1993

CREDITS

Architect of Record
Susan Maxman Architects
123 South 22nd Street
Philadelphia, Pennsylvania
19103

Architectural Consultant
John Dickey, FAIA (deceased)

Structural Engineer
Ortega Consulting
Media, Pennsylvania

Architectural Historians
Alice Kent Schooler
West Chester, Pennsylvania

Professor Bernard Herman
Newark, Delaware

General Contractor and Mason
James D. Groff
Christiana, Pennsylvania

*Prime Interior Finish and Structural
Carpentry*
Chandlee Carpentry
West Grove, Pennsylvania

*Roofs, Windows, and Structural
Carpentry*
James Stoner
Paradise, Pennsylvania

Photographer
Catherine Bogert
Philadelphia, Pennsylvania

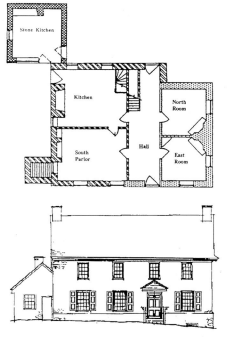
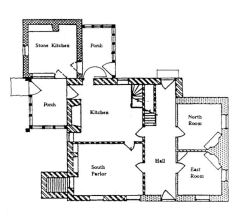

Sketch of the house, 4-Bay Georgian Plan as established by 1800-1812.

Elevation sketch showing recent additions c. 1989 - 1994.

Restoration of 18th Century Farmstead

Floor Plans / Elevations

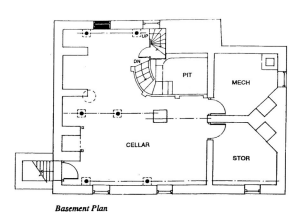

Basement Plan

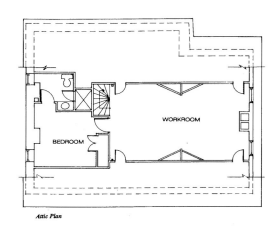

Attic Plan

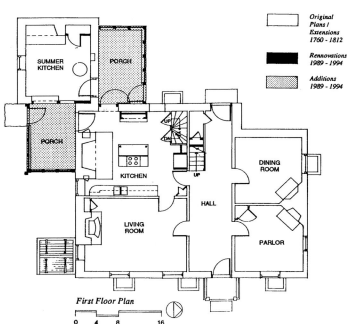

	Original Plans / Extensions 1760 - 1812
■	Rennovations 1989 - 1994
▨	Additions 1989 - 1994

SUMMER KITCHEN

PORCH

PORCH

KITCHEN

DINING ROOM

UP

HALL

LIVING ROOM

PARLOR

First Floor Plan

0   4   8   16

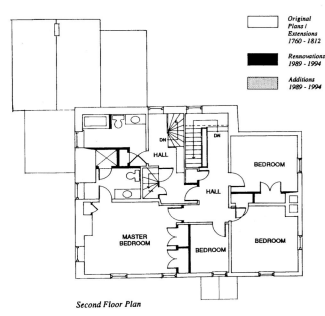

	Original Plans / Extensions 1760 - 1812
■	Rennovations 1989 - 1994
▨	Additions 1989 - 1994

DN

DN

HALL

BEDROOM

HALL

MASTER BEDROOM

BEDROOM

BEDROOM

Second Floor Plan

State of Utah Governor's Mansion

Salt Lake City, Utah

MJSA Architecture

ARCHITECT'S STATEMENT

The historic Thomas Kearns Mansion, the official governor's residence for the State of Utah, was built in 1902 and gutted by fire in 1993. The limestone structure in French Chateau style features High Victorian interiors. Restoration required the complete documentation and removal of interior elements; smoke removal and deodorization of all cavities; and conservation, restoration, and replication of carved wood elements, plaster and composition ornamentation, decorative finishes and carved stone. Mechanical and electrical systems were replaced, a fire-suppression system added, and a seismic upgrade performed. The family quarters were redesigned for privacy and safety.

OWNER
State of Utah Division of Facilities Construction and Management

DATA

Type of Facility
Governor's residence

Type of Construction
Restoration

Historic Status
National Register of Historic Places
Contributing structure in a National Register Historic District
Contributing building in local historic district

Area of Building
20,000 GSF

Total Project Cost
$7.8 million

Status of Project
Completed July 1996

CREDITS

Architect of Record
MJSA Architecture
357 West Pierpont Avenue
Salt Lake City, Utah 84101

Structural Engineer
Tanner Willmore Smith and Associates
Salt Lake City, Utah

Mechanical Engineer
Olsen and Peterson Consulting Engineers Inc.
Salt Lake City, Utah

Electrical Engineer
BNA Consulting Engineers
Salt Lake City, Utah

Architectural Conservation
Thom Gentle Associates
Stamford, Vermont

Deodorization and Cleaning
Martin Churchill Associates, Inc.
Arlington, Virginia

Interior Design
Ellie Sonntag Interior Design
Salt Lake City, Utah

Contractor
Culp Construction Company
Salt Lake City, Utah

Photographer
Richard Springate
Seattle, Washington

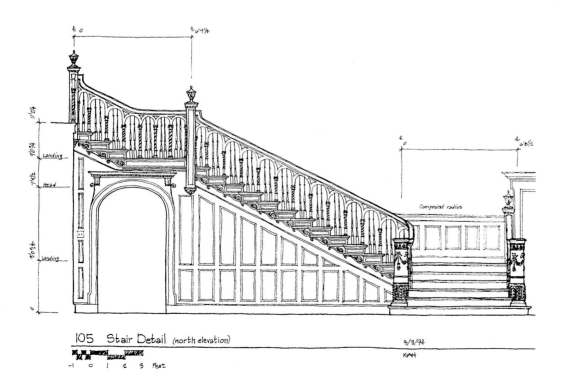

105 Stair Detail (north elevation)

-1 0 1 2 3 Feet

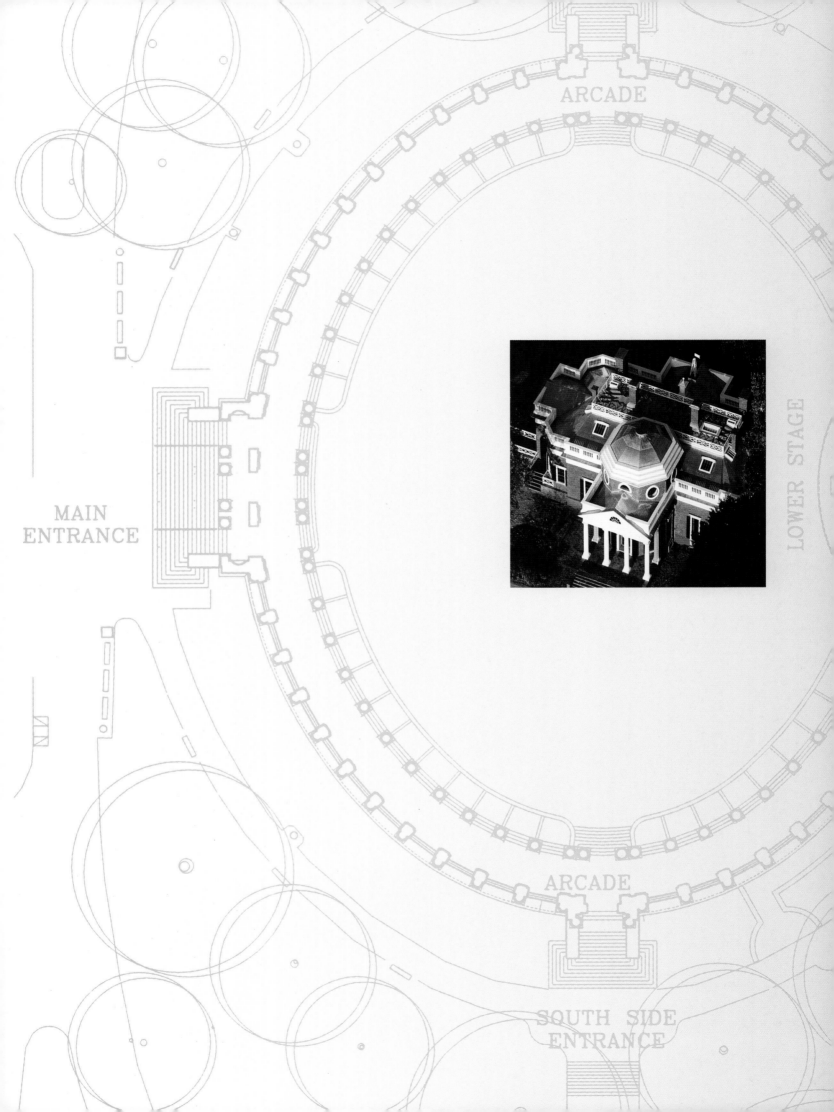

MAIN
ENTRANCE

ARCADE
ENTRANCE

LOWER STAGE

ARCADE

SOUTH SIDE
ENTRANCE

NORTHEAST
ENTRANCE

NORTH OB
DE

RECEPTION
BUILDING

Special Projects

PER STAGE

TOMB OF THE
UNKNOWN
SOLDIER

SOUTH OBSERVATION
DECK

SITE PLAN

Memorial Amphitheater, Arlington National Cemetery
Arlington, Virginia

Einhorn Yaffee Prescott, Architecture & Engineering, P.C.

ARCHITECT'S STATEMENT

The Memorial Amphitheater, designed by Carrere and Hastings and built between 1915 and 1920, serves as a ceremonial monument at Arlington National Cemetery. The structure has suffered from chronic moisture- and water-related problems throughout its history. A study was undertaken to identify the causes of structure and site problems and to provide cost-effective design solutions. The scope included development of a building history, a physical investigation coupled with nondestructive and laboratory testing to identify construction deficiencies and in-situ cleaning tests.

The challenge was to develop waterproofing and roofing systems to accommodate the building's thermal movement and allow water drainage from behind stones. More than 400 drawings and 43 different treatments were developed to restore stone elements. Sympathetic accessibility modifications were made to the box seats and site.

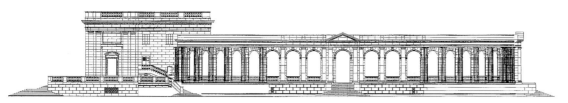

NORTH ELEVATION

EAST ELEVATION

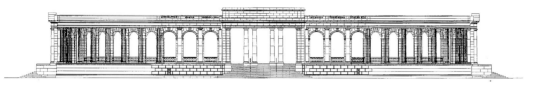

WEST ELEVATION

0   8'   16'   32'

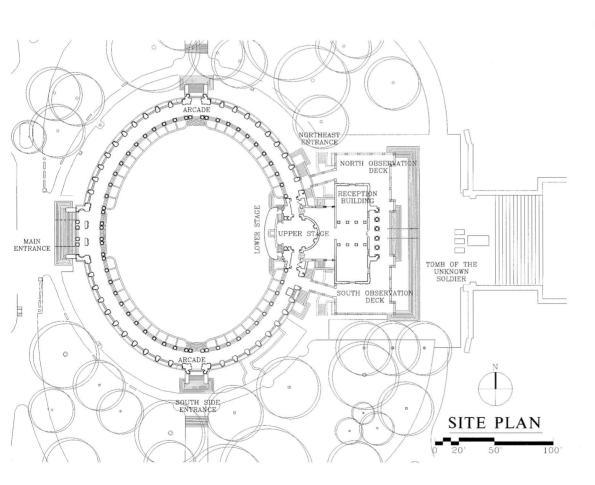

SITE PLAN

0   20'   50'   100'

OWNERS
U.S. Army Corps of Engineers,
Baltimore District

DATA
Type of Facility
Ceremonial monument

Type of Construction
Restoration

Historic Status
National Register of Historic
Places

Area of Building
65,000 GSF

Total Project Cost
$12 million

Status of Project
Completed May 1996

CREDITS
Architect of Record/
Mechanical/Electrical Engineer
Einhorn Yaffee Prescott,
Architecture & Engineering, P.C.
1000 Potomac Street, N.W.
Washington, D.C. 20007

Structural Engineer
McMullan & Associates
Vienna, Virginia

Waterproofing Consultant
Seal Engineering
Alexandria, Virginia

Landscape Architect
Stephenson & Good
Alexandria, Virginia

Contractor
Clark Construction
Bethesda, Maryland

Photographer
Walter Smalling, Jr.
Washington, D.C.

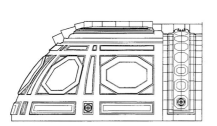

SECTION-STAGE CEILING

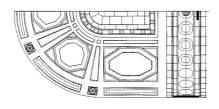

REFLECTED CEILING PLAN

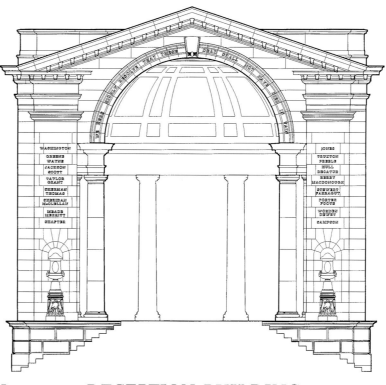

RECEPTION BUILDING
WEST ELEVATION

The Biltmore Hotel
Coral Gables, Florida

Barry Berg Architect

ARCHITECT'S STATEMENT

A National Historic Landmark, the Biltmore Hotel in Coral Gables, Florida, opened in 1926. After its extraordinary Romanesque lobby, the Country Club Ballroom is the most significant public space in the hotel complex. As part of an extensive renovation, five monumental Moorish chandeliers, missing since World War II, had to be re-created. Full-sized fabrication drawings were based on a period photograph found in the city archives. Laser-cutters and scrolling machines were used to replicate the intricate arabesque ornamentation in bronze-patinated aluminum. An unanticipated effect of the new chandeliers is the projection of the pierced patterns on the walls.

OWNER
City of Coral Gables
Leased by Seaway Biltmore
Hotel

DATA
Type of Facility
Hotel

Type of Construction
Restoration

Historic Status
National Historic Landmark

Total Project Cost
$75,000

Status of Project
Completed January 1994

CREDITS
Architect of Record
Barry Berg Architect
1200 Anastasia Avenue
Coral Gables, Florida 33134

Structural/Mechanical/Electrical Engineer
David Volkert & Associates, Inc.
Miami, Florida

Lighting Designer
Jeffrey Harris
Miami, Florida

Decorative Painted Ceiling Restoration Consultants
Paul Fullerton, Josefina Larrain
Miami, Florida

Manufacturer
La Spec Industries, Inc.
Los Angeles, California

Photographer
Tom Burt
San Diego, California

Illustrated Guidelines for Rehabilitating Buildings at the Presidio of San Francisco

Golden Gate National Recreation Area, California

Architectural Resources Group, Architects, Planners, & Conservators, Inc.

ARCHITECT'S STATEMENT

The *Illustrated Guidelines for Rehabilitating Buildings at the Presidio of San Francisco* is intended to serve as a detailed, site-specific document to guide future planners, architects, tenants, and compliance reviewers in considering proposed treatments of historic structures and sites at this National Historic Landmark just south of the Golden Gate Bridge.

Established by the Spanish in 1776, the Presidio has played a prominent role in the U.S. Army since the 1840s. On January 1, 1995, the Presidio was transferred from the Department of Defense to the Department of the Interior. The National Park Service, which is fully responsible for the facility, is currently involved in a long-term planning process to develop guidelines for activities and land use consistent with preserving the history and natural resources of the Presidio. Many of the buildings are, or will be, occupied by new tenants, and as many as 315 new buildings will be leased to the private sector. The new guidelines merge the language, general requirements, and format of the U.S. Secretary of the Interior's *Standards for Rehabilitation* and the *Illustrated Guide for Rehabilitating Historic Buildings* with the specific issues and concerns of the Presidio. The resulting document is useful for training and compliance purposes beyond the specific project level.

OWNER
Presidio Project Office, Golden Gate National Recreation Area

DATA

Type of Facility
Historic military post

Type of Project
Special project

Historic Status
National Historic Landmark Contributing structure in a National Register Historic District

Total Project Cost
Not applicable

Status of Project
Completed March 1995

CREDITS

Architect of Record
Architectural Resources Group, Architects, Planners, & Conservators, Inc.
Pier 9
The Embarcadero
San Francisco, California

Production Management
Backen Arrigoni & Ross, Inc.
1660 Bush Street,
San Francisco, California

Graphic Design and Publication Services
William Barrett Graphic Design & Advertising
Point Reyes Station, California

Photographer
Stephen J. Farneth, AIA
San Francisco, California

Internal Revenue Service Headquarters Building

Washington, D.C.

Karn Charuhas Chapman & Twohey

ARCHITECT'S STATEMENT

The objective of this project was to complete the two unfinished facades of the Internal Revenue Service Headquarters Building in a manner appropriate to its style and consistent with the Federal Triangle Master Plan. Both facades were located between dissimilar exteriors never intended to be seen together—a public facade facing the street and a private interior courtyard. The new design replicates the style and materials of the existing public facades, matching the stone coursing and details, fenestration, and roofline. Significant design and technical challenges were resolved by a simplified expression of the entrance in recognition of the limited plaza space and in the use of three different methods of stone erection.

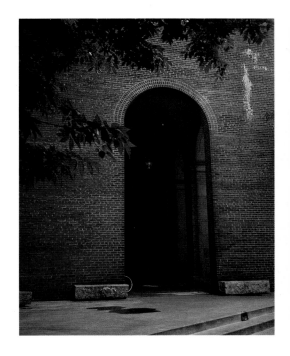

OWNER
General Services
Administration

DATA
Type of Facility
Federal office building

Type of Construction
New facade construction

Historic Status
Contributing structure in a
National Register Historic
District

Total Project Cost
$6.1 million

Status of Project
Completed December 1993

CREDITS
Architect of Record
Karn Charuhas Chapman
& Twohey
1150 17th Street, N.W.
Suite 103
Washington, D.C. 20036

Structural Engineer
Johns & Bhatia
Bethesda, Maryland

Mechanical/Electrical Engineer
Grotheer & Company
Washington, D.C.

Civil Engineer
Wiles Mensch Corporation
Reston, Virginia

Landscape Architect
Coffin and Coffin
Washington, D.C.

Contractor
Charles H. Tompkins Company
Washington, D.C.

Photographer
Hoachlander Photography
Associates
Washington, D.C.

Monticello

Charlottesville, Virginia

Mesick Cohen Wilson Baker Architects, LLP

ARCHITECT'S STATEMENT

Monticello served as Thomas Jefferson's "architectural laboratory" for nearly sixty years. Even the roofscape was evolving throughout his lifetime. With a compound configuration of pitched and serrated surfaces clad in sheet iron, tinplate, lead, and copper, the roof was freighted with thirty skylights, six chimneys, a weathervane tower, a gong house, more than 300 feet of classical balustrade, an ornamental Chinese railing, and the first dome on an American dwelling. In the century and more after his death in 1826, these features were repeatedly modified, and many were lost. In commemoration of the 250th anniversary of

Jefferson's birth, the roof, as he knew it, was restored to Monticello.

Three years of archival research, in-situ investigation, construction of mock-up assemblies, and preparation of a historic structure report culminated in the preparation of construction documents. To ensure a century of life for the restored roof, a rubber membrane was placed under metal cladding, and stainless steel was substituted for the historic sheet iron. Tin was custom plated onto stainless steel to replicate original tin shingles. All roof features were reinstalled using 200-year-old assembly techniques.

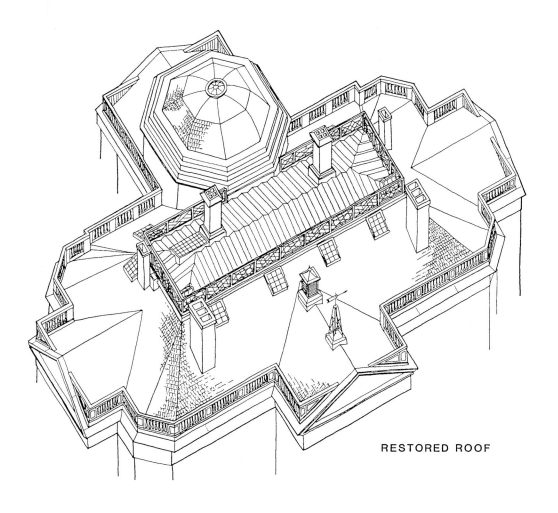

RESTORED ROOF

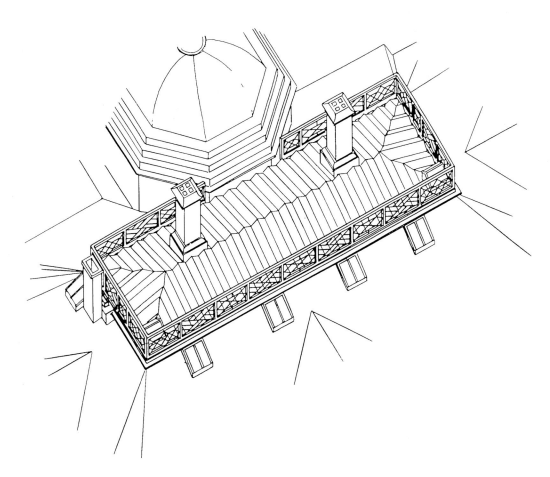

OWNER
The Thomas Jefferson
Memorial Foundation

DATA

Type of Facility
House museum

Type of Construction
Restoration

Historic Status
National Historic Landmark
Inscribed on the UNESCO World
Heritage List

Area of Building
18,800 GSF

Total Project Cost
$1 million

Status of Project
Completed 1991

CREDITS

Architect of Record
Mesick Cohen Wilson Baker
Architects, LLP
324 Broadway
Albany, New York 12207

Contractor
Henry N. Lewis Contractors, Inc.
Owings Mills, Maryland

Photograph Credit
Original image courtesy of
Monticello/Thomas Jefferson
Memorial Foundation, Inc.
Gift of Vincent P. Rubera
Photographed by Jim Carpenter

Mount Vernon Treading Barn
Mount Vernon, Virginia

Quinn Evans/Architects

ARCHITECT'S STATEMENT

This replica of George Washington's famous sixteen-sided barn (circa 1792) is the centerpiece of the new Pioneer Farmer exhibition at Mount Vernon. The barn represents the creative agricultural pursuits of the nation's first president, and the first time the grain-treading process was undertaken indoors. Supplied with only a glass-plate slide taken circa 1870, a list of the original construction materials, and the structure's overall diameter (52 feet), the architects were able to create a historically accurate reconstruction. As a permanent addition to the estate's living-history exhibits, the integration of a modern foundation system, electrical services, concealed structural reinforcements, and provisions for accessibility were also key elements in the project's development.

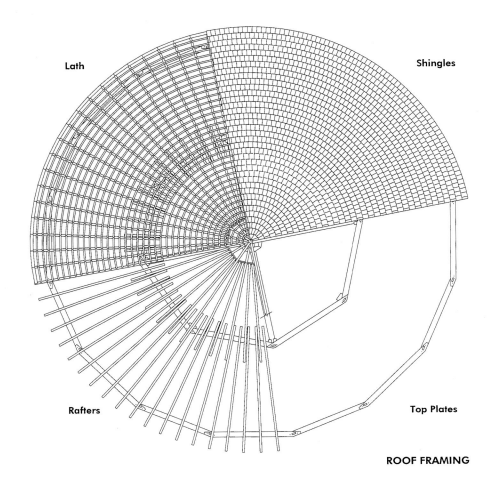

Lath

Shingles

Rafters

Top Plates

ROOF FRAMING

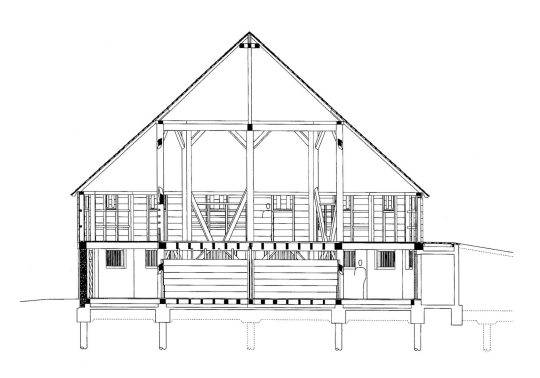

OWNER
Mount Vernon Ladies'
Association

DATA
Type of Facility
Living-history exhibit

Type of Construction
Special reconstruction

Historic Status
Re-created structure in
National Historic Landmark
complex

Dimension of Building
4,250 GSF

Total Project Cost
$1.5 million (construction only)

Status of Project
Completed September 1996

CREDITS
Architect of Record
Quinn Evans/Architects
1214 28th Street, NW
Washington, D.C. 20007

Structural Engineer
McMullan & Associates
Vienna, Virginia

Mechanical/Electrical Engineer
Smith & Faass Consulting
Engineers
Germantown, Maryland

Historians
Orlando Ridout, V
Annapolis, Maryland

William Graham
Petersburg, Virginia

Lighting Consultant
Coventry Lighting
Washington, D.C.

Contractor
John O'Rourke
Solomons, Maryland

Photographers
Larry Olsen
Washington, D.C.

Mount Vernon Ladies'
Association
Mount Vernon, Virginia

Plum Street Temple
Cincinnati, Ohio

Piaskowy & Keller, P.S.C., Architects and Planners

ARCHITECT'S STATEMENT

Plum Street Temple is not only a treasure for Reform Judaism, but is also an architectural and historic gem for the citizens of Cincinnati. It was placed on the U.S. Department of the Interior's Register of Historic Places in 1972 and was designated a National Historic landmark in 1975.

Phase I restoration work included replacement of all roofing, reinforcement of the structure, restoration of windows, repair of metal work, installation of attic ventilation and wiring, and installation of a new glass balcony railing. Phase II entailed repair of all decorative plaster and restoration of the entire stenciled interior. More than 100 new stencils were cut, and more than forty custom paint colors were blended to match the original stencils and colors. All sanctuary lighting was replaced or refurbished, and an up-to-date sound system was installed.

OWNER
Isaac M. Wise Temple

DATA

Type of Facility
Synagogue

Type of Construction
Restoration

Historic Status
National Historic Landmark
State and local landmark

Area of Building
25,000 GSF

Total Project Cost
$2 million

Status of Project
Completed July 1995

CREDITS

Architect of Record
Piaskowy & Keller, P.S.C.,
Architects and Planners
14 East Eighth Street
Covington, Kentucky 41011

Structural Engineer
Steven Schaefer Associates, Inc.
Cincinnati, Ohio

Mechanical Engineer
Lee Grosser Associates, Inc.
Highland Heights, Kentucky

Electrical Engineer
Herndon Engineering Services, Inc.
Milford, Ohio

Acoustics Consultant
Richard J. Lemker & Associates
Covington, Kentucky

Painting and Plaster Restorationist
Evergreene Painting Studios, Inc.
New York, New York

Contractor
Warm Brothers Construction
Company
Cincinnati, Ohio

Photographer
J. Miles Wolf
Cincinnati, Ohio

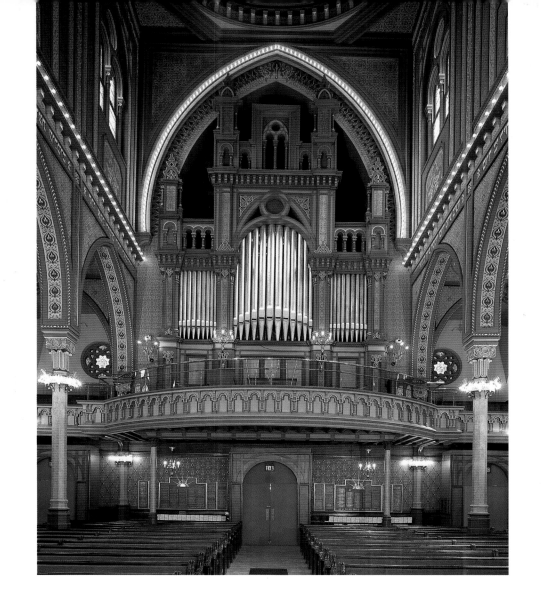

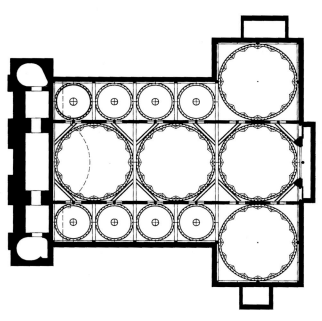

REFLECTED CEILING PLAN

0 10 20   40 FEET

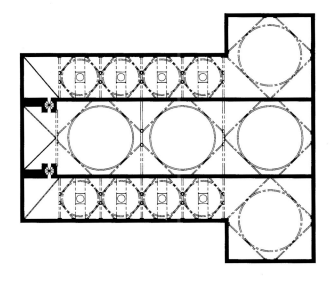

ATTIC PLAN

0 10 20   40 FEET

Poplar Forest
Forest, Virginia

Mesick Cohen Wilson Baker Architects, LLP

EAST ELEVATION

ARCHITECT'S STATEMENT

Poplar Forest, Thomas Jefferson's classically inspired retreat constructed outside Lynchburg, Virginia, in 1806, is considered one of his most brilliant architectural achievements. After the house was devastated by fire in 1846, a later occupant reconstructed it as a simple Greek Revival farmhouse using surviving portions of the original brickwork. The house remained largely unaltered until 1984, when it was purchased by a local citizen. When alterations and finishes were removed, valuable evidence of Jefferson-period details and finishes was exposed. Findings gleaned from above- and below-ground archeology and from intensive study of the Jefferson archives and contemporary Jeffersonian buildings constituted the basis of an exhaustive historic-structure report, which thoroughly studied all of the period construction details and assemblies that were later incorporated into the construction documents. The exterior of the house is now being painstakingly restored using late-eighteenth- and early-nineteenth-century construction technology.

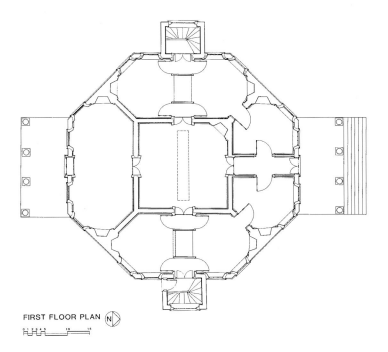

FIRST FLOOR PLAN (N)

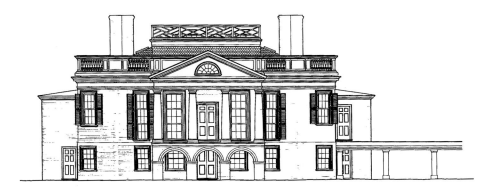

SOUTH ELEVATION

BUILDING SECTION LOOKING EAST

OWNER
  The Corporation for Jefferson's
  Poplar Forest

DATA
  Type of Facility
  House museum

  Type of Construction
  Restoration

  Historic Status
  National Historic Landmark

  Area of Building
  4,650 GSF

  Total Project Cost
  $3 million

  Status of Project
    Estimated date of completion:
    November 1997

CREDITS
  Architect of Record
    Mesick Cohen Wilson Baker
    Architects, LLP
    324 Broadway
    Albany, New York 12207

  Structural Engineer
    Klepper Hahn & Hyatt
    East Syracuse, New York

  Contractor
    The Corporation for Jefferson's
    Poplar Forest
    Forest, Virginia

Thomas Jefferson's Academical Village, University of Virginia

Charlottesville, Virginia

James Murray Howard, Ph.D., FAIA

ARCHITECT'S STATEMENT

Ongoing preservation and restoration (1984–2025) of Thomas Jefferson's Academical Village (1817–1826) constitute a curatorial program of research, archeological investigation, craft training, and preservation education unique among World Heritage List sites. State-of-the-art restoration has been conducted at five of the seventeen original structures. Advanced technologies used to address the Americans with Disabilities Act, cutting-edge metallurgic technology, and modern building systems allow the precinct to be a living historic property that is free of the damage common to such places. The work has received state, national, and international recognition for its use of enlightened institutional stewardship in preserving the national patrimony.

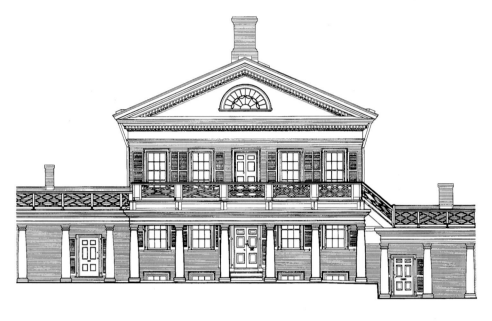

0   5   10   20 FEET

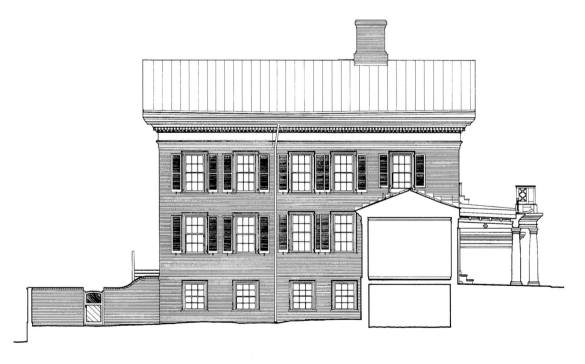

Top, west elevation

Bottom, north elevation

OWNER
University of Virginia/
Commonwealth of Virginia

DATA
Type of Facility
University historic district

Type of Construction
Special project

Historic Status
National Historic Landmark
National Register Historic
District
Inscribed on the UNESCO World
Heritage List

Area of Site
28 acres

Total Project Cost
$7 million through 1996

Status of Project
Ongoing

CREDITS
Architect of Record
James Murray Howard,
Ph.D., FAIA
Curator and Architect for the
Academical Village
575 Alderman Road
Charlottesville, Virginia 22903

*Consultant for Historic Structure
Reporting, Roofing, and Barrier-Free
Access*
Mendel Mesick Cohen Waite
Hall Architects
Albany, New York

Mechanical/Electrical Engineer
Paul A. Sweet, P.E., RA
Richmond, Virginia

Fire-Protection Engineer
Schirmer Engineering
Corporation
Deerfield, Illinois

(credits continue)

Credits (continued)

Landscape Research and Access Consultant
   EDAW, Inc.
   Alexandria, Virginia

Barrier-Free Access Consultant
   Barrier Free Environments
   Raleigh, North Carolina

Contractor
   University of Virginia Facilities
   Management
   Charlottesville, Virginia

Photographer
   Michael Bailey Photography
   Charlottesville, Virginia

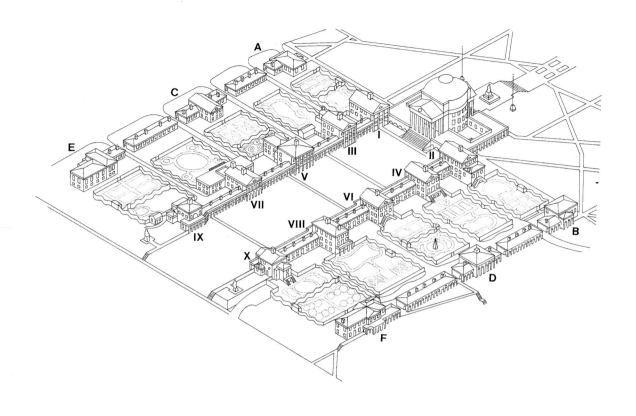

State Capitols

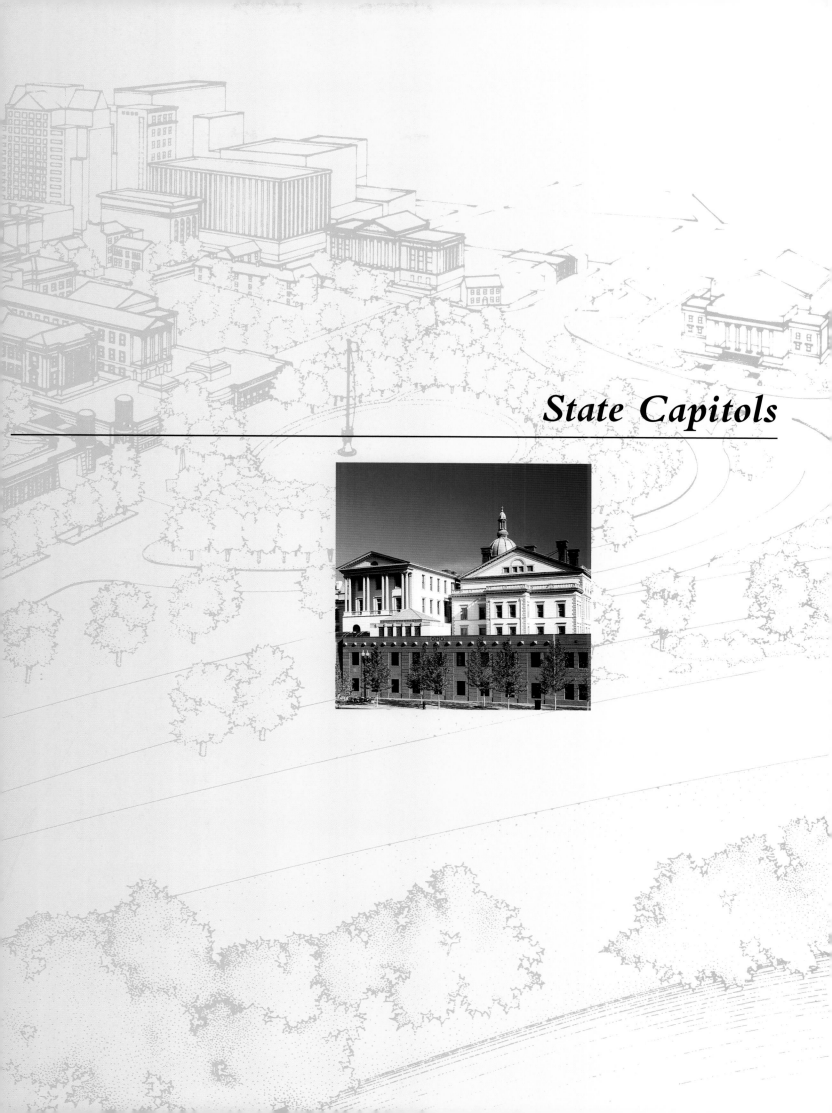

Michigan State Capitol
Lansing, Michigan

Wigen, Tincknell, Meyer & Associates, Inc.

ARCHITECT'S STATEMENT

Restoration of the Michigan State Capitol was accomplished in twelve phases by three architectural firms coordinated by a preservation architect. Restoration included the upper corridors, rotunda, House of Representatives Chamber and House offices.

The state capitol was restored to its original splendor while preserving its function as a working state capitol. The building was retrofitted with new heating/ventilation/air conditioning and electrical systems, technology wiring, and plumbing. Chandeliers appropriate to the capitol were custom fabricated for all offices and public spaces. Decorative plaster and extensive decorative painting were reinstated based on careful research of original painting. Woodwork was wood-grained in keeping with the original construction.

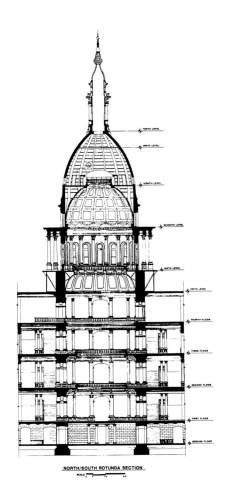

NORTH/SOUTH ROTUNDA SECTION

OWNER
State of Michigan

DATA
Type of Facility
State capitol

Type of Construction
Restoration

Historic Status
National Register of Historic
Places

Area of Building
89,439 GSF

Total Project Cost
$22 million

Status of Project
Completed November 1993

CREDITS
Architect
Wigen, Tincknell, Meyer &
Associates, Inc.
1647 South Washington Avenue
Saginaw, Michigan 48601

Restoration Architect
Richard Frank, FAIA
302 East Henry Street
Saline, Michigan 48176

Structural Engineer
Robert Darvas & Associates
Ann Arbor, Michigan

Mechanical/Electrical Engineer
SWS Engineers, Inc.
Southfield, Michigan

Acoustical Consultant
Jaffe, Holden, Scarbrough
Acoustics, Inc.
Norwalk, Connecticut

(credits continue)

Credits (continued)

Lighting Consultant
Gary Steffy Lighting Design
Ann Arbor, Michigan

Decorative Painting Consultant
Darla Olson
New York, New York

Contractor
The Christman Company
Lansing, Michigan

Photographer
Dietrich Floeter Photography
Traverse City, Michigan

New Jersey State Capitol

Trenton, New Jersey

Ford Farewell Mills & Gatsch/Johnson Jones—Joint Venture Architects

ARCHITECT'S STATEMENT

The design team prepared a master plan for the New Jersey Statehouse complex and its archeologically sensitive site, and made code and technological improvements to the legislative wing of the Statehouse, parts of which date from 1792. The Assembly Chamber (1892) and Senate Chambers (1903), as well as other key historic spaces, were preserved and restored. A compatible 30,000-square-foot addition created a ceremonial entrance and office space. The 165,000-square-foot Statehouse Annex was fully renovated to house the Office of Legislative Services and seventeen legislative hearing rooms. A new 1,500-car garage replaced surface parking and will allow for the re-creation of Stacy Park behind the Statehouse.

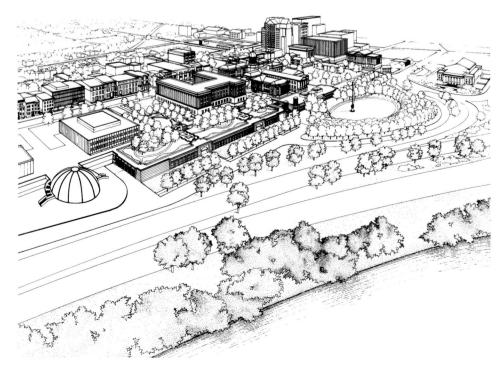

OWNER
    State of New Jersey

DATA
Type of Facility
    State capitol

Type of Construction
    Restoration and rehabilitation

Historic Status
    National Register of Historic
    Places
    State landmark

Area of Buildings
    270,000 GSF

Total Project Cost
    $106.3 million

Status of Project
    Phase I completed October 1991
    Phase II completed February 1995

CREDITS
Architect of Record
    Ford Farewell Mills &
    Gatsch/Johnson Jones—Joint
    Venture Architects
    864 Mapleton Road
    Princeton, New Jersey 08540

Structural Engineer
    Blackburn Engineering/French
    and Parrello
    Manalapan, New Jersey

*Mechanical/Electrical/Plumbing and
Fire-Protection Engineer*
    Joseph R. Loring Associates, Inc.
    New York, New York

Geotechnical Engineer
    French and Parrello Associates, P.A.
    Holmdel, New Jersey

Paint Analysis Consultants
    Frank Welsh
    Bryn Mawr, Pennsylvania

    Biltmore Campbell Smith
    Restorations, Inc.
    Asheville, North Carolina

(credits continue)

Credits (continued)

Materials Conservation Consultant
Building Conservation
Associates, Inc.
New York, New York

Stained Glass Conservation
Consultant
McKernan Satterlee
Associates, Inc.
Brewster, New York

Archeological Consultant
Hunter Research
Trenton, New Jersey

Photogrammetry Consultant
Dennett Muesig Ryan,
Associates
Iowa City, Iowa

Specificier
Robert Schwartz, RA
New York, New York

Construction Managers
Lehrer McGovern and Bovis
(Phase I)
Princeton, New Jersey
Turner Construction (Phase II)
Trenton, New Jersey

Photographers
Otto Baitz/Esto
Mamaroneck, New York
Brian Rose
New York, New York
Elton Pope-Lance
Sudbury, Massachusetts

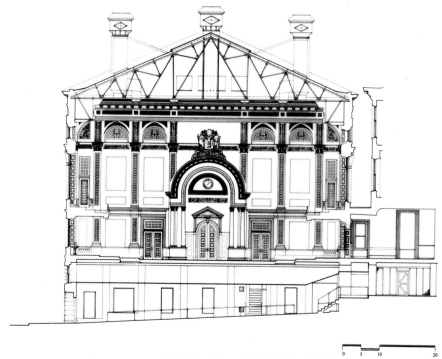

ASSEMBLY WING: TRANSVERSE SECTION

0   5   10   20

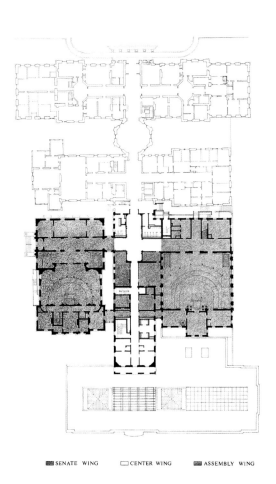

■■■ SENATE WING   ☐ CENTER WING   ■■■ ASSEMBLY WING

Pennsylvania State Capitol

Harrisburg, Pennsylvania

Vitetta Group

ARCHITECT'S STATEMENT

Modeled after St. Peter's Basilica in Rome, this 1906 landmark has undergone uninterrupted restoration since 1981. The architectural team's investigation and research for the client included physical evaluation and forensic assessment of existing conditions, moisture-management studies, construction documentation, and cost estimation. Carefully researched restoration efforts have reversed years of neglect and have returned selected areas to their original grandeur while maintaining public access. Restoration and renovation planning included updating the building's mechanical, electrical, and life-safety systems and designing a data/communications fiber-optic network for the State House of Representatives. Restored spaces to date include the main entrance, public corridors, offices and elevators, the State Supreme Court dome, the House and Senate galleries, and Senate support spaces. Selected marble interiors have been cleaned, including the main rotunda.

OWNER
Commonwealth of Pennsylvania

DATA
Type of Facility
State capitol

Type of Construction
Restoration

Historic Status
National Historic Landmark

Area of Building
503,908 GSF

Total Project Cost
$13 million

Status of Project
Ongoing

CREDITS
*Design and Master Planning
Architect/Structural/Mechanical/
Electrical Engineer*
Vitetta Group
642 North Broad Street
Philadelphia, Pennsylvania
19130

Contractors
G&W Contracting
Hummelstown, Pennsylvania

Cumberland Contracting
Harrisburg, Pennsylvania

Albert Michaels Conservation
Harrisburg, Pennsylvania

Bob Smith Contractors
Maytown, Pennsylvania

Herre Brothers
Enola, Pennsylvania

Photographers
Hunt Commercial Photography
Dillsburg, Pennsylvania

Joanne Bening
Philadelphia, Pennsylvania

Tom Crane Photography
Bryn Mawr, Pennsylvania

Texas State Capitol

Austin, Texas

3D International, Inc. and Ford, Powell & Carson, Inc.—Joint Venture

ARCHITECT'S STATEMENT

The restoration of the 100-year-old Texas State Capitol building challenged the architectural team to fulfill the requirements of a modern office/legislative building while relieving dangerous overcrowding and the architectural diminishment that had resulted from years of neglect and inappropriate modification. Construction of a below-grade extension provided additional space with minimal impact on the historic building and grounds. Removal of intrusive elements revealed the original historic interior spaces and allowed for their restoration. Mechanical, electrical, plumbing, and state-of-the-art communications were integrated into the building in concert with a distinctive glass-and-wood partition system containing air-conditioning equipment, coffee bars, and storage that allowed spaces requiring subdivision to remain visibly intact.

The metal dome roof, skylights, masonry, wood doors and windows, and exterior porches and lanterns were restored. Missing elements were replicated from remaining elements and existing documentation.

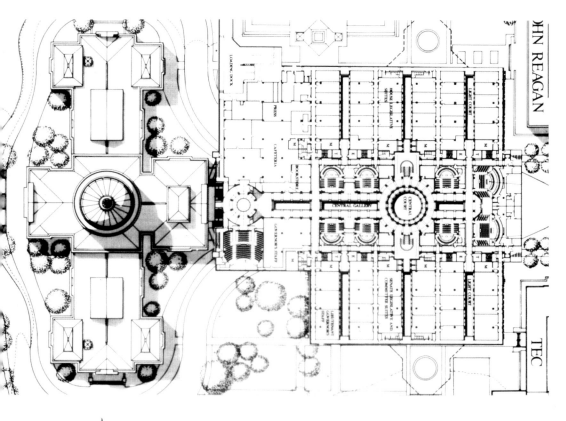

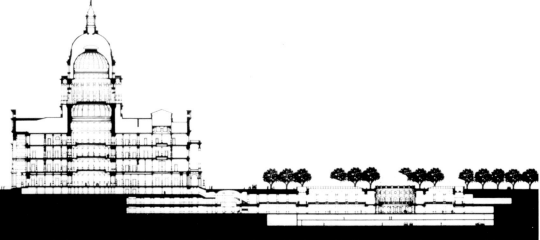

OWNER
State of Texas

DATA

Type of Facility
State capitol

Type of Construction
Restoration and rehabilitation

Historic Status
National Historic Landmark
State landmark

Area of Building
384,600 GSF

Total Project Cost
$152.8 million

Status of Project
Completed March 1995

CREDITS

Architect of Record
3D International, Inc. and Ford, Powell & Carson, Inc.—
Joint Venture
1138 East Commerce Street
San Antonio, Texas 78205

Project Architect
Ford, Powell & Carson, Inc.
1138 East Commerce Street
San Antonio, Texas 78205

Structural Engineer
The Datum/Moore Capitol—
Joint Venture
Austin, Texas

Mechanical/Electrical Engineer
Carter & Burgess, Inc.
Fort Worth, Texas

Landscape Architects
Fly Associates, Inc./Ford, Powell & Carson, Inc.
San Antonio, Texas

Graphic Designer
Fuller Dyal & Stamper
Austin, Texas

Preservation Technology Consultant
Volz & Associates
Austin, Texas

(credits continue)

WEST ELEVATION

Transportation

Amtrak's 30th Street Station

Philadelphia, Pennsylvania

Dan Peter Kopple & Associates

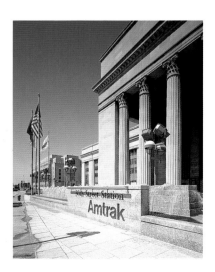

ARCHITECT'S STATEMENT

Amtrak's 30th Street Station is a historic landmark that has been faithfully restored to its original grandeur while new building systems and amenities have been integrated into the building's historic fabric. The rehabilitation project has cleaned and refinished the interior and exterior, renovated all 250,000 square feet of the upper four floors of offices to contemporary standards, created a new food and retail market in the original shopping area, converted unused mail-handling areas into a 430-car garage, and provided dramatic new site improvements. Additionally, night illumination has brought life and added safety to the immediate area.

OWNER
  30th Street Limited, L.P.

DATA
  Type of Facility
  Railroad station

  Type of Construction
  Restoration and rehabilitation

  Historic Status
  National Register of Historic
  Places
  State landmark

  Area of Building
  500,000 GSF

  Total Project Cost
  $82 million

  Status of Project
  Completed June 1991

CREDITS
  Architect of Record
  Dan Peter Kopple & Associates
  421 Chestnut Street
  Philadelphia, Pennsylvania 19106

  *Structural/ Mechanical/Electrical
  Engineer*
  The Kling Lindquist
  Partnership, Inc.
  Philadelphia, Pennsylvania

  Contractor
  The George Hyman Construction
  Company
  Bethesda, Maryland

  Owner's Representative
  Gerald D. Hines Interests
  Houston, Texas

  Photographer
  Bob Golding
  B & H Photographers
  Philadelphia, Pennsylvania

Angels Flight™ Railway
Los Angeles, California

Tetra Design, Inc.

ARCHITECT'S STATEMENT

Angels Flight,™ "the shortest railway in the world," was constructed in 1901 as a funicular to transport the residents of Bunker Hill to and from the city's booming commercial and financial districts below. This landmark of iconic significance to generations of Los Angeles citizens bridges the new and the old. The historic stationhouse is sensitively juxtaposed onto the podium extension of the modern high-rise water court, setting the stage to experience the historic wooden incline cars, concrete trestle, tracks, and historic arch below. The restoration of this historic rail system completes a critical section of downtown's pedestrian linkages plan, connecting new urban development with the historic core.

OWNERS
Angels Flight™ Railway
Foundation

DATA

Type of Facility
Funicular railway

Type of Construction
Rehabilitation

Historic Status
Local landmark
City historic-cultural monument

Total Project Cost
$4.1 million

Status of Project
Completed February 1996

CREDITS
Developer
Community Redevelopment
Agency, City of Los Angeles
Los Angeles, California

Architect of Record
Tetra Design, Inc.
1055 Wilshire Boulevard
Suite 1885
Los Angeles, California
90017-5602

Construction Manager
Harris & Associates
Concord, California

Historic Restoration Consultant
Historic Resources Group
Hollywood, California

Structural Engineer
Krakower Associates
Arcadia, California

Mechanical Engineer
The Sullivan Partnership
Glendale, California

Electrical Engineer
Pacific Engineers Group
North Hollywood, California

Contractor
Pueblo Contracting Services
San Fernando, California

Photographer
Bielenberg Associates
Los Angeles, California

Danville Rail Passenger Station

Danville, Virginia

Wood Swofford & Associates, Architects

ARCHITECT'S STATEMENT

The first project completed in the Commonwealth of Virginia under the Intermodal Surface Transportation Efficiency Act (ISTEA), Transportation Enhancements Program, this rehabilitation exemplifies the spirit of the motivating legislation and sets the standard for all future historic rail station renovations. Following the U.S. Secretary of the Interior's *Standards for Rehabilitation*, the facility was renovated and finishes were restored for the combined use as an Amtrak rail passenger station and a regional science center. The completed restoration interprets the building's circa 1922 appearance. The interpretation, resulting from an in-depth survey of the building's cultural resources, features the building as the nucleus of the Historic Tobacco Warehouse and Residential District.

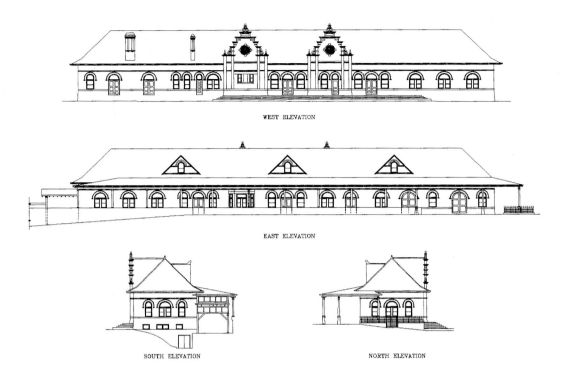

WEST ELEVATION

EAST ELEVATION

SOUTH ELEVATION

NORTH ELEVATION

OWNER
City of Danville

DATA
Type of Facility
Science center, museum, and
Amtrak station

Type of Construction
Rehabilitation

Historic Status
National Register of Historic
Places
Contributing structure to a
National Register Historic
District

Area of Building
16,000 GSF

Total Project Cost
$1.2 million

Status of Project
Completed December 1995

CREDITS
Architect of Record
Wood Swofford & Associates,
Architects
812 East High Street
Charlottesville, Virginia 22902

Mechanical/Electrical Engineer
Brandt Engineering, Inc.
Richmond, Virginia

Landscape Architect
Hill Studios, P.C.
Roanoke, Virginia

Finishes Conservation Consultant
Sara B. Chase
Lexington, Massachusetts

Lead/Asbestos Consultant
Imec Engineers
Lynchburg, Virginia

Contractor
John W. Daniels & Company
Danville, Virginia

Photographer
Michael Compson
Compson Studios
Danville, Virginia

Depot Plaza
Lafayette, Indiana

HNTB Corporation

A R C H I T E C T ' S   S T A T E M E N T

The Big Four Depot, built in 1902, had ceased to function as a train depot. The railroad relocation project in Lafayette provided the opportunity for the depot to serve as an intermodal passenger station and to provide meeting space, office space, and ticketing for Amtrak and the Lafayette bus system. Relocating the depot four blocks north and raising it a full story created challenges in accessibility, queuing for the train and buses, and for plaza events. The project also provided for the creative reuse of the Main Street Bridge as a linear plaza and pedestrian link between two municipalities.

OWNER
   City of Lafayette

DATA
   Type of Facility
   Intermodal transportation
   facility and community plaza

   Type of Construction
   Rehabilitation and special
   project

   Historic Status
   Eligible for the National
   Register of Historic Places

   Area of Building
   11,000 GSF

   Total Project Cost
   $7.3 million

   Status of Project
   Completed March 1996

CREDITS
   Architect of Record/
   Structural/Mechanical/
   Electrical Engineer
      HNTB Corporation
      111 Monument Circle,
      Suite 1200
      Indianapolis, Indiana 46204

   Associate Architect
      Blitch Architects, Inc.
      757 Charles Avenue
      New Orleans, Louisiana 70130

   Contractor
      Walsh Construction Company
      of Illinois
      Chicago, Illinois

   Photographer
      Gary Quesada
      Korab Hedrich Blessing
      Chicago, Illinois

Reading Terminal Train Shed at Pennsylvania Convention Center

Philadelphia, Pennsylvania

Thompson, Ventulett, Stainback & Associates

ARCHITECT'S STATEMENT

Philadelphia's Reading Terminal Train Shed, constructed between 1891 and 1893, ceased to operate in 1984. The adaptive reuse of the shed, along with the new exhibition building built in 1993, comprise the Pennsylvania Convention Center. Preservation of the train shed also saved the Reading Terminal Market, a lively and picturesque cultural landmark.

The renovated train shed houses the convention center's ballroom, some meeting rooms, and a grand hall that preserves the original volume of the vast interior. The ballroom is separated acoustically from the grand hall by a glass partition, the design of which echoes the existing glass wall at the south end of the shed and allows views between the grand hall and the ballroom. Inlaid stainless steel strips in the terrazzo floor recall train tracks, and marble-clad pylons housing mechanical supply and uplighting reference the bumpers that stopped the trains. Visitors will enter the complex through the Reading Terminal's historic headhouse, which fronts on Market Street, then progress to the grand hall and across a bridge to the exhibit building.

OWNER
Pennsylvania Convention
Center Authority

DATA

Type of Facility
Convention center

Type of Construction
Restoration, rehabilitation,
and special project

Historic Status
National Historic Landmark
Listed on the state and local
registers of historic sites

Area of Buildings
1.36 million GSF (convention
center)
166,000 GSF (shed)

Project Cost
$212.5 million (convention
center construction)
$65 million (shed, including
$10 million for market)

Status of Project
Completed March 1994

CREDITS

Architect of Record for Design
Thompson, Ventulett, Stainback
& Associates
2700 Promenade Two
1230 Peachtree Street, N.E.
Atlanta, Georgia 30309

Architect of Record
Vitetta Group
The Wallace Building
642 North Broad Street
Philadelphia, Pennsylvania
19103

Structural Engineer
Ross Bryan Associates, Inc.
Nashville, Tennessee

Mechanical/Electrical Engineer
PWI Engineering, Inc.
Philadelphia, Pennsylvania

Historic Consultant
Vitetta Group
Philadelphia, Pennsylvania

(credits continue)

Credits (continued)

Interior Design
Design Services, Inc. and
Thompson, Ventulett, Stainback
& Associates—Joint Venture
Philadelphia, Pennsylvania
Atlanta, Georgia

*Acoustics/AudiovisualSound System
Consultants*
Acentech, Inc.
Cambridge, Massachusetts

Architectural Lighting Design
Grenald Waldron Associates
Narberth, Pennsylvania

Contractor
Dick Incorporated
Pittsburgh, Pennsylvania

Photographer
Brian Gassel
Thompson, Ventulett, Stainback
& Associates
Atlanta, Georgia

Index of Architects